Our world doesn't need another book; it needs an idea
that could change the course of history. Write with us.

A CIP catalogue of this book is available from the National Library of Australia.

Flynn, Daniel
Chapter One

ISBN 978-0-9943109-7-2

Published and project managed by The Messenger Group Pty Ltd
PO Box H241, Australia Square NSW 1215

This book is published on FSC paper.

Editing by Sarah Megginson, Tara Francis, Hannah Easton and Sarah Prescott
Proofreading by Jen Taylor
Book Design by Wesley Rodricks and Tia le Clercq
Photography by Kim Landy, Jason Lau, Sebastian Avila and Shelley Morris

For PR, marketing and speaking opportunities, contact hello@thankyou.co

DEDICATION

This book is dedicated to you. On behalf of the Thankyou team, I want to offer our sincerest gratitude for your contribution to impacting global poverty.

It's unusual to find a book dedicated to you, isn't it? Surely this book can't be dedicated to all of the readers, can it? Is it just an obvious attempt at flattery? Far from it. Without the support of every single person who has participated in Thankyou's journey - whether you've bought one bottle of water, stocked your cupboards full of our products or invested in this book - we have you to thank.

You may have been part of building this story with us for many years, or you may have just recently joined us. Either way, we are so pleased to have you on board as we embark on an epic journey together. This dedication isn't flattery. It's our small attempt to honour you all, because this book has been written with you, by you and about you - and for that, we thank you.

Thanks Justine, Jarryd, Sarah, Hannah, Wesley, Jan-Lee, Bethany and The Messenger Group for your work in putting together a world-first book concept.

Daniel Flynn

CONTENTS

CHAPTER 1.1 The Game Just Changed / **09**

CHAPTER 1.2 The Journey Begins / **29**

CHAPTER 1.3 Turning Stumbling Blocks Into Stepping Stones / **52**

CHAPTER 1.4 The 'Why' Behind What You Do / **75**

CHAPTER 1.5 High-Five The Status Quo In The Face – With A Chair / **91**

CHAPTER 1.6 Build A Great Team To Achieve A Great Dream / **108**

CHAPTER 1.7 Facing The Giants / **128**

CHAPTER 1.8 The Campaign That Changed It All / **147**

CHAPTER 1.9 Money Doesn't Change Everything / **170**

CHAPTER 1.10 The Four-Letter Word: Fear / **190**

CHAPTER 1.11 Partnering With Dreamers, Believers And Haters / **205**

CHAPTER 1.12 Playing Hide-And-Seek In The Dark / **214**

CHAPTER 1.13 Choose Remarkable / **236**

TESTIMONIALS

If ever there was a book that deserved and was destined to be the new #1 best-seller, 'Chapter One' is it. It's amazing.
- Steve McKnight, best-selling author and property investment expert

Thankyou's remarkable story shows the power of social enterprise. It's a tale that will inspire all generations and motivate you to get out and make a difference in your own special way.
- David Koch, TV personality and business commentator

Young, bold, brave, full of heart and, unquestionably, one of the smartest marketers I have had the privilege of working with. This book will not only teach you profound new things, but leave you reassessing exactly what you were put on this planet for.
- Lisa Messenger, founder and editor-in-chief of *The Collective*

In a world full of challenges and complexities it is too easy to underestimate the power that each one of us holds to change things for the better. Daniel Flynn is someone who lives out the values of a deeply-held faith in the future and the will to get great things done. This is a book for everyone... all of us need to remind ourselves that we can, as Gandhi said, be the change we want to see. We need to see every challenge as an opportunity, every setback as a chance to learn and do better. Daniel's story and ideas, his infectious enthusiasm and his limitless sense of possibility, will challenge you, encourage you and motivate you to find your own dream and pursue it with passion.
- Tim Costello, CEO of World Vision Australia

There are many who aspire to change the world, but few have have done so with the passion, focus and humility of Daniel Flynn. This book is as inspiring as it is empowering.
- Michael McQueen, business trends expert and 2015 Australian keynote speaker of the year

Daniel, Justine and Jarryd are breaking the mould... They are disruptors, without even knowing it; they used common sense and tenacity to not only start their business but also to grow it to where it is today. Steve Jobs said, "The ones who are crazy enough to think that they can change the world are the ones who do". Aptly named, *Chapter One* is just the start of the Thankyou journey I think Daniel is that crazy. I cannot wait to see what *Chapter Two* has in store.
- Janine Allis, founder of Boost Juice

Thankyou epitomises the Bobby Kennedy quote, "There are those who look at things the way they are, and ask why... I dream of things that never were, and ask why not?" In its journey to date, Thankyou has challenged people's definition of what is possible and shown the unshakable power of purpose-driven people and business models. This is Chapter One of a game-changing story that will defy your plot expectations, challenge your assumptions and ultimately leave you uplifted and empowered. Just wait for Chapter Two...
— **Holly Ransom, keynote speaker and CEO of Emergent Solutions**

Daniel Flynn is a rare breed who thinks differently, turning the world upside down and inside out in order to make it a better place. This book is a manifesto that may just change the world...
— **Darrell Wade, co-founder of Intrepid Travel**

Thankyou has emerged with breath-taking speed and ambition to become one of the most exciting brands within the global social enterprise movement. The highest commitment to quality, the disruptive and fearless approach to marketing, the audacious ambition and the incredible positive impact it has on the world... Thankyou isn't just good. It is the future.
— **Peter Holbrook, CEO of Social Enterprise UK**

The world needs, more than ever, people who can re-imagine the future and get to work making it happen. Within this book is the magic to live your life on purpose and make the world a better place.
— **Jack Delosa, managing director of The Entourage**

Raw and real, Daniel's story will challenge your thinking. Thankyou is a force of change to be reckoned with.
— **Petra Bagust, media personality and director at HP Media Ltd**

Bold, inspiring and impactful, this book explores the age-old saying – if you always do things the way you've done them you'll always get the same result. We need change and more importantly, we need agents of change. If this is the warm up act, I can't wait for the main show.
— **Don Meij, group CEO and managing director of Domino's Pizza Enterprises Ltd**

Entrepreneurs make a habit of shaking things up and showing what can be done with a combination of inspiration and perspiration. What Daniel Flynn and the Thankyou team has achieved is monumental, and all the more unique because all of the gains go to those who really need a hand. This book is a unique exploration of what it takes to really make a difference: buy a copy for everyone you know – for the insights, and for the outcomes.
— **Craig Winkler, co-founder of MYOB, entrepreneur and philanthropist**

Thank you Daniel Flynn for making the impossible feel possible... start a successful retail business, reduce global poverty, create a social cause that changes the world – no problem! This is a book about pushing boundaries. It teaches you how to see things differently, it challenges you to test convention, to notice the world's limitations and not only wonder why they exist, but ask what you can do about them. Pay what you want, but invest in a movement that also invests in you. Grow with it, be inspired and change a few million people's lives along the way!

– Alisa Camplin, motivational speaker and Olympic gold medallist

The amazingly simple idea of Thankyou being the vehicle that enlists a whole generation to be game changers and lift the burden of crushing poverty from the lives of millions of people is the inspiring journey of this book. Daniel makes it possible for all of us to be the change.

– George Savvides, CEO of Medibank

This book challenges convention, but more importantly, it challenges us. Thank you Daniel Flynn for thinking differently, for truly changing the world and for allowing us to be a part of the next chapter. We can change the world. We just need to think differently.

– Mike Green, managing director of Harcourts International Ltd

What the Thankyou team does is never settle. Not because a company brand book tells them not to, but because the fire to do so lives within their gut. They are a group of like-minded people crazy enough to think that we just might be able to solve some issues, change the world or just leave it in a better place than we got it.

– Travis Garone, founder of Movember

I have been working with social enterprises for the last 10 years and the next chapter of Thankyou is the most inspiring, courageous and game changing approach I have seen. Thankyou will be transformational in our society, create social good and inspire a new generation of social entrepreneurs globally.

– Lisa Waldron, executive officer of the Westpac Foundation

Daniel Flynn has changed the game of benevolence and social responsibility. He has it all; a revolutionary and brilliant businessman whose charisma and selflessness has allowed him into the world's most influential companies; a digital genius who's created remarkable change through online platforms; and a true humanitarian whose generous spirit has empowered people to give many millions of dollars to those less fortunate. Watch this space.

– Barry Markoff, founder and managing director of Australasia's largest speaking bureau, ICMI

CHAPTER 1.1
The Game Just Changed

*I want to introduce you to something
that you've most likely never seen before.*

RIGHT WAY OR WRONG WAY UP?

On the surface this book appears like it's written and formatted the 'wrong way around'. Now, if that were all there was to it, this design would be nothing more than an annoying gimmick. But I promise that once you read a little further you'll understand why this book had to be printed like this, and you'll also discover that the minute you purchased this book you became part of a movement that I believe will change the world we live in. I hope you're ready to read on.

I write this book knowing full well that our world doesn't need another book. There are already enough inspirational, motivational and educational books available, many written by well-respected and highly credible authors. Readers are spoilt for choice and another story for the sake of another story cluttering the shelf simply isn't needed.

So, you might be wondering, "Why this book, then?"

Our world doesn't need another book, but it does need us to wake up to the realisation that we have the power to change everything. This is a world-first book concept that will stretch you and challenge you in ways books haven't before.

For seven years now, I've been invited to speak publicly about a little idea I had at the age of 19. I've walked into schools, universities and corporate offices to share the story with different people from all walks of life. Many times when I've arrived to speak to grade one or two students, I've felt apprehensive that the story wouldn't resonate or that the ideas and concepts would be too complex for them to understand. But I left those engagements stunned and surprised as these kids responded to the Thankyou story with statements like, "One day I want to work with you" and "One day I want to change the world."

I've walked into high schools where the teachers warned, "These kids won't respond, so don't let it throw you." I would begin the Thankyou story and watch as these non-responsive kids sat wide-eyed, right on the edge of their chairs, and throughout my talk they would laugh, smile, some would even cry, leaving their teachers speechless at how the tale of our journey held their attention.

I have found myself in front of university students, wondering if it's going to matter when they find out I haven't actually got a degree. I remember walking in to speak to some of our nation's most elite sporting personalities, having made an unfounded assumption that they might not relate to my talk. I was a little star-struck by some of the people in the room, and even more surprised later to hear that their overwhelming response to the story was that it was the best talk they'd ever had at the club.

Speaking at corporate conferences in Australia, New Zealand and around the world, alongside founders and CEOs of billion-dollar empires, Olympians, TV personalities and some of the most inspiring people you'd ever meet, I have felt like I didn't fit in with this crowd. Did I really have that much to offer, to share the stage with this calibre of people? As I reflected on these things one day, I asked myself: "In what room does this story fail?" A short time later, I was convinced I had found that room.

On my way to deliver a keynote presentation, I stood in the lift in my skinny jeans, T-shirt and blazer – my standard speaking attire. I looked at the other people in the lift with me and wondered where they all might be going. They were dressed in bow ties and ballgowns. A little dressy for a Thursday evening, I thought. The lift arrived at the floor I had been directed to and to my horror, as I exited, the bow tie-clad, ballgown-wearing folk followed my lead. Right at that point it felt like my heart stopped.

Attention to detail isn't my thing. As the event organiser looked me up and down in a mix of confusion and shock, it hit me. The event was black tie. It all came rushing back to me – this was the talk I was going to be doing "in a few weeks" to "one of the most prestigious rooms you could be invited to".

I found myself at table number one, where the speaker sits, visually offending a few hundred Australian directors. The gentleman on my left sat on 25 boards, while the woman across from me had won Australian Director of the Year. This was, by far, the most senior room I'd ever presented to.

And so, I figured I'd found it – a room where the story wouldn't work. As I was introduced to the stage, my stomach was turning and my mouth was dry. I stood before a room of the movers and shakers of industry and our society. I stood, vulnerable, underdressed and completely unsure whether anything I had to say had any value to this room of leaders.

As I talked, they laughed – harder than most groups laugh. I figured that they were laughing at me, not with me. The 'amateur antics' of a kid with a few friends taking on the largest multinationals in the world would sound pretty funny to a group of people like this. Especially when much of our organisation's journey challenges the way things have always been done.

But what happened at that keynote caught me completely off guard. Later that night there were queues of people wanting to connect me with various colleagues, or thanking me for my time and for sharing my "wisdom". Wisdom? What wisdom could I possibly offer such a prestigious room of successful people?

WHERE IT ALL BEGAN

'The story' began when I got a couple of friends, including my best mate and then girlfriend (now wife) together to talk about starting an organisation that I dreamed would challenge the very fabric of the capitalist global business model. It was a bold idea, especially for a group of kids with no money, no qualifications and almost no experience in business.

But it seems we were onto something. Years later, a group of our staff were attending an industry event and the former managing director of Kellogg's Australia and New Zealand, a man with global experience and recognition, told the entire event that our organisation was "the Apple of the fast-moving consumer goods industry". He was later quoted in an article saying that in his 31 years of international experience working in big blue chip companies, he had never seen a team seize an opportunity and execute a communications campaign as successfully as our organisation had.

For myself and my other co-founders, Jarryd and Justine, along with our team who have all spent time sharing our story, we have been humbled to see our journey inspire many – and in turn we've been inspired by the many who have partnered with us to see our dream become a reality.

For years now I have been told, "one day you should write a book". The key phrase being "one day". I always pictured that time existing far out in the future, because tradition would say you write the book once you've 'made it', so to speak. We haven't made it.

You're meant to write the book once your idea has scaled globally, and ours hasn't. If you want your book to sell well, you write the book once hundreds of millions of people know about you, and that's not the case with us – yet.

You're meant to write the book once the dream is a reality. But instead, everything you are about to read is only our warm-up act.

CHAPTER ONE

I'm about to share 'the story' with you, but before I do, I promised I'd show you something you haven't seen before. Brace yourself, because it's a little unconventional.

This book is titled *Chapter One* because it's the first chapter of our story. Instead of waiting until our journey is finished, I decided to write this book as we go, chapter by chapter. Books are usually written in full hindsight and retrospect that cover decades of a person's individual or corporate journey; they're often full of insights and inspiration, but they can also be unrelatable. Sometimes after reading them, I'm left feeling like I could never attain that sort of success in my life.

This book is written as we go, to show you that any one individual, any group of people, can make their ideas and dreams a reality. You may not have 'made it' yet (and neither have we), but everything we have learned along the way we want to share with you, in the hope that it will encourage you, inspire you and empower you.

Now I'm going to make an assumption. I'm going to assume that for every book you've ever read you have only ever played the role of the reader. You buy the book, you start reading it and you become the reader, simple right? So history would tell us, because that is the way things have always been done before.

But this book challenges that position. It challenges the norm in more ways than just the print orientation of the design. You see, the moment you picked up this book you became more than a reader. You became a social investor. Part of a group of like-minded souls, philanthropically investing their money into an idea that could change the course of history. Like I said at the start of this book, our world doesn't need another book – but it does need ideas that will change it forever.

That is what this book aims to be, as 100 per cent of the profit from *Chapter One* will fund the future of our story: our eventual *Chapter Two*. And by 'Chapter Two', I'm not only referring to the physical production of a second book, but the next stage of the Thankyou journey that a second book will (hopefully) document.

But what on earth are you investing in? I'm glad you asked!

WE ARE THANKYOU

Around 1 billion people are living in extreme poverty[1] (World Bank, 2014). Nearly 6 billion people aren't. I'm not sure what your views are on global poverty, but, personally, I've always been overwhelmed by the big statistics. To an individual person, 1 billion can seem like a big number. But often what we don't consider is that 6 billion people don't live in extreme poverty. Put in this context, all of a sudden that first number gets a little smaller.

Every day billions of us pour tens of billions of dollars into consumer products, which line the pockets of the world's largest multinationals. I, on my own, probably can't do much, but what if we – the collective consumer – could? What if all of us together could take the billions we are already giving to multinationals every day and make better choices to help impact those still without access to basic human rights? Herein lies the potential game changer.

Many years ago, I had an idea. What if there was a brand, a collection of consumer goods, that could empower consumers and give them a choice between the big multinationals, who exist to profit shareholders, and a brand that existed 100 per cent to fund life-changing aid and development programs for people living in extreme poverty? I had never heard of a social enterprise that existed 100 per cent for impact (no shareholder interest) that had achieved a market-leading position.

Enter Thankyou, a social enterprise. What started out as an idea in 2008 in Australia among a few university students, led to a small business launched from my parents' garage, which has now grown into a thriving enterprise that has gained incredible momentum.

At this moment in time, there are more than 35 products under the Thankyou brand across multiple product ranges, including breakfast cereals, snack bars, bottled water, hand and body wash, hand lotion, soap and sanitiser. Our water range exists 100 per cent to fund water projects; our food ranges exist 100 per cent to fund food programs; our body care products exist 100 per cent to fund health and sanitation projects – all with the aim of empowering communities around the globe. We work with our impact partners to implement cutting-edge development projects. I'll explain a bit more about our impact model later on in the book.

Our products are stocked in the major supermarkets – Coles, Woolworths, IGA, Foodland, La Manna – of our home country, Australia, as well as in 7-Eleven Australia, Starbucks Australia, Australia Post, Chemmart Pharmacies, Ben and Jerry's Australia, and thousands of other independent outlets.

We've carried out disruptive marketing campaigns that have gained worldwide attention and have seen us achieve things multinationals (who, unlike us, have multimillion-dollar marketing budgets) haven't managed to. The results have stumped many industry experts and have demonstrated the force of a people-powered brand.

In our short history, we've appeared in over 700 stories and features in print and broadcast press, and we've built an online community of hundreds of thousands of people. Australians have gotten behind our brand, helped us spread the word, and purchased tens of millions of Thankyou products.

We've set out to create remarkable products, because if the products were average, you and I (the consumer) would probably buy them once for the cause and then go back to buying the brands we usually use. Some of our products have the highest loyalty rates in the supermarket and outsell multiple global competitors, all of which has helped us move towards our driving goal: to play a significant role in eradicating extreme poverty.

We've raised millions of dollars and, through our aid and development impact partners, we've funded sustainable projects across 16 countries and impacted the lives of hundreds of thousands of people all around the globe.

But this…

This is just the beginning.

PROOF OF CONCEPT

Enter Chapter Two, which involves new product ranges and new markets. But it begins with the launch of 'FutureFund by Thankyou', which is essentially a crowdfunding platform we've set up to – wait for it – fund the future of our organisation. Instead of just asking you to donate to the fund, we bring you this book, where 100 per cent of the profit goes to the 'FutureFund by Thankyou'. The fund has many milestones to reach and the most exciting bit is that you, a movement of empowered people, get to be involved like never before – writing with us, building with us and growing with us, with the ultimate driving goal being to eradicate global poverty.

The first funding milestone is to launch the Thankyou baby and toddler product range that will exist 100 per cent to fund infant and maternal health programs in developing countries.

Children between the age of birth and five years are the most vulnerable in poor communities – each year almost 3 million young children don't make it to their first month – largely because of preventable issues (WHO, 2014). On top of that, every 90 seconds a mother in childbirth loses her life (WHO, 2015). This range will exist to change both of those facts.

But that's just the first milestone.

Everything within the story you will read in this book has been part of creating 'proof of concept'. We've proven that this idea can start in a country from the ground up, successfully challenging some of the biggest brands in the world. We've proven a model that ultimately leads to making a remarkable impact in the lives of those living in extreme poverty.

The second milestone: to launch Thankyou New Zealand. The second part of 'proof of concept' is seeing whether Thankyou can start in another country from the ground up and scale.

Why New Zealand? We want to empower New Zealanders, the way we've empowered Australians, to show the world that consumers have the power to change stuff. Many of the biggest brands in the world trial ideas in New Zealand because it's widely known that if a concept works in New Zealand, it will work globally. So we've invited New Zealand to help take this movement to the next level.

The thing is, we're not just launching Thankyou Australia into New Zealand. Instead, we're launching Thankyou New Zealand from scratch. We'll be setting up a local team, local suppliers and local impact partners. Coinciding with this book arriving on shelves, we launched our boldest and most ambitious campaign yet, inviting both Australians and New Zealanders to make a choice – to either help launch Thankyou New Zealand or not to.

Will it work? We can't guarantee that it will. But I love this thought: if it does, then together two of the smallest countries in the world (at times underestimated), who both bat above their weight globally in sport, entertainment and music, could go on to do something the likes of which the world has never seen before.

If together we can reach that milestone and successfully launch into a new market, then what next? Maybe one day you'll find it written about in a book called *Chapter Two*.

As this book keeps selling, the 'FutureFund by Thankyou' will keep growing (we hope). You can track the progress and funding updates at *thankyou.co*. New funding targets will be set to help us reach bolder and even more ambitious goals. But we can't build the future of Thankyou on our own; we need you.

WHY DO WE NEED YOU?

According to traditional thinking, our idea was flawed from the very start. Thankyou exists 100 per cent for impact. How our business model works is that after all the costs involved in making great products are taken care of, every cent left over funds life-changing projects. We can make that claim because Thankyou has no individual shareholders and our business that sells the products, pays the staff and all the other expenses involved in building the brand is owned 100 per cent by our own Charitable Trust (our only 'shareholder'). Every quarter, we distribute our profits to the Charitable Trust and 100 per cent of these funds are paid out to our impact partners, who implement the work in the field.

When brands want to expand into new markets (like a new country) and launch new ventures (like our new baby and toddler range) they seek out investment from investors to finance the growth. But at Thankyou we have no investors. This is awesome because it allows us to keep our 100 per cent claim but it also presents a challenge in that it limits our potential to grow fast!

How serious are we about this 100 per cent claim? You could walk up to us with a \$300 million cheque for any percentage share in Thankyou and we'd kindly thank you for your enthusiasm, but we wouldn't and couldn't take it. You can't buy a stake in Thankyou and if you ask any start-up expert, this decision has ruled out our ability to scale up and take Thankyou to where we know it's going to go.

We are taking a different path because we want consumers to be able to choose a brand that exists 100 per cent for impact. And we're inviting you to join us so that together we can write the future of Thankyou, with the aim of impacting millions of lives.

It sounds a little crazy to be scaling an organisation from funds generated by the sale of a book. Especially when book retailers and publishers are going bankrupt and books – don't make a whole lot of money. With that in mind, why are we inviting you to fund the future of Thankyou through the purchase of a book?

For us, it's not about the money itself (although we need that). It's about buy-in.

We don't have the millions or billions of dollars that our global competitors have to develop flashy marketing campaigns for our product. The power of Thankyou works most powerfully when millions of people understand the concept. There are only so many hours in a day where I, or another team member, can get up and share the story and vision in front of an audience. This book provides the ability for the story to be told and for the vision to be shared far and wide. This is why we need to get this book in as many hands as possible.

As you read about our '100 per cent for impact' model and our call out to people to play a part in funding the future of the organisation, you could wonder if us co-founders at the helm of Thankyou might change our minds if and when offers come in to take Thankyou global. But those offers have already come in, and we have already said no (you'll read about them later on).

We are serious at Thankyou about our game-changing model. There isn't a successful example that has grown to where we plan to take this, and we know the road to get there is going to look very different to one that's ever been travelled before. It doesn't mean other models are wrong, they are just not right for Thankyou.

We've never been afraid to go where no one's gone before, to get a result no one's got before. We've never been afraid to challenge the status quo as we take our ideas and make them a reality.

Herein lies our gift to you. This book isn't just a tool we are using to get a story out and to fund the future of Thankyou together, to impact millions of people globally. This book is also a tool for you personally, or your team or your organisation, to help make your ideas and dreams a reality. My hope is that this tool will motivate and equip you to shake up what everyone once thought was possible and completely change the game.

FLIP ONE THING; CHANGE EVERYTHING

As I was driving one day, I had a thought: "Why aren't books written landscape? Why are they always vertical with text left to right?" These are somewhat random, pointless questions. For many reasons, I could have and possibly should have just let those questions come in and out of my mind and moved on. But for many greater reasons, I couldn't afford to. And neither can you.

I know that to make your ideas and dreams a reality, you cannot afford to accept things as they are. You will have to challenge your thinking, regularly. There is a good chance that you just read over that sentence quickly, and could therefore easily make the mistake of missing the significance of it. I could have put it in bold, but I still questioned if it would really sink in. So, I wondered… What if I didn't just tell you? What if every time you picked up this book, your thinking was challenged?

As simple as it is to flip this book around, it challenges us, as we are all used to reading 'the other way'. Maybe there's a part of you that is thinking about putting this book down, such is your frustration at absorbing this unusual format.

But who knows? If you keep reading and allow yourself to move past the mental boundaries of 'the way you've always done it', you might start to wonder why more books aren't printed like this. You might realise that it's actually easier to hold, because as you rest it on your leg or table, you free up the use of one hand, as it's not needed to support the weight of the book. Or, what if you discover you can read faster? Why is it that when we read a Microsoft Word or a Pages document we scroll top to bottom yet when it comes to books we read left to right?

The answers to these questions are not even that important. What is important is that once you get out of your comfort zone, you begin to actually ask questions – and you start thinking and challenging what you've always accepted as the norm. The reality is that stepping out is uncomfortable. Even as you read this book 'the wrong way around' in airport lounges, on public transport, on your way to school or work or around friends, there's a chance you'll feel uncomfortable.

Why? Because there is the possibility that people will notice you are doing something differently. We live in a world where we can blend in fairly easily, that is until the moment you take a risk and attempt something that perhaps no one has done before.

As you read, you'll probably discover that flipping the page up is at first uncomfortable. It's different and unconventional, but within that action lies the answer to this question: do you have what it takes to push through and do something you've never done before? To change things, you must become comfortable in the uncomfortable.

I had to risk your discomfort (knowing you may walk away from this book and never hear our story) and my discomfort, because if each of us could truly understand the value of challenging our thinking and start to question the way things have always been done, our world and our lives would look completely different.

Why is it uncomfortable from our end? The concept of the horizontal book goes against the grain of everything that's been done in publishing books in this genre. Think about it. There's the fact that online retailers, for instance, present digital thumbnails in a vertical aspect, and nearly every bricks and mortar book retailer configures their physical shelf space to display books vertically, not horizontally. As our team researched horizontal books, we discovered that any previous attempt had succeeded at failing!

There is not one book on the bestsellers list that is printed in this format. Since the beginning of commercial book sales, not just millions but billions of readers have become used to the way things have always been done. We live in a society that, based on the above facts, would define the very format of this book to be 'wrong'. There are too many systems, processes and industry standards in place that make it impossible. The status quo has been set. If you want to release a successful, best-selling book, it would seem smart to do it the way it's always been done, to follow a proven formula.

But just because there isn't a successful example, that doesn't mean an idea or concept is destined to fail... Does it?

THE GAME JUST CHANGED

At Thankyou our journey hasn't just been about our ideas and dreams becoming a reality. It's been a story of changing the game, from entering a capitalist market with a social model through to the unconventional ways we have marketed our products and brand. The very concept of changing the game is both exciting and terrifying.

I believe that if you don't change the game someone else will. That's an invitation to challenge established ideas because we can never afford to get comfortable in doing things how they've always been done. And it's a call to generate new ideas because innovation opens possibilities that we never knew existed.

This book was published in 2016, a year when the largest taxi company in the world owned no actual vehicles: Uber. A year when the largest accommodation provider in the world owned no physical buildings or property assets: Airbnb. These companies have allowed everyday drivers and homeowners to become taxi service and accommodation providers, respectively. They disrupted two of the most established markets in global commerce because they realised that they had the power to change stuff. Then, they challenged the way things have always been done – and they made a massive impact as a result. Wind the clock back a decade and try and explain to an industry expert that this shared economy model would become a driving force within a few short years, spitting out several billion-dollar enterprises. They would have called you crazy.

The moral of the story? Some people don't think the game will ever change. But it always does. And if you aren't convinced the game will change, it's probably best to keep those thoughts to yourself, otherwise years later you might find yourself mentioned in a quote like this: "The iPhone is nothing but a niche product" – then-CEO of Nokia in 2008.

The launch of *Chapter One* is another attempt at changing the game. Not because it's printed horizontal (although that's a point of difference) but because while our competitors put their faith in their multimillion- (and multibillion-) dollar investors, we put our faith in you to fund the future. We've really flipped the publishing game on its head by not only launching in an unusual format, but also by releasing this book without a recommended retail price. Instead of stipulating an RRP, we launched the book with 'pay what you want'. We did this knowing that you could pay $1 for the book... but also wondering, what if someone paid $10,000? (We've got to dream big, right?)

We feel that by launching with this unique model, the question is no longer, "How much do you want to pay for this book?" Instead it becomes, "How much are you willing to invest into an idea that could change the course of history?" Everyone who purchases this book, no matter what price they pay, will be contributing to a cause that makes a significant and lasting impact against global poverty. We can't wait to see how this plays out!

I should mention we didn't just limit this pricing strategy to our online store. Twenty-four hours after meeting with a global leader and Australia's largest book retailer, LS Travel Retail – they own Relay, Newslink and Watermark, with stores in every airport in Australia and New Zealand – we realised we'd found a bold partner willing to change the game with us. They've stepped up to become the first retailer to launch this world-first book concept, selling it at the retail level with a 'pay what you want' price tag. Can you think of another book to be sold through a retail chain, where you could walk up to the counter and name the price?

The most significant part of this deal wasn't the "yes" that we received from LS Travel Retail (although that was undeniably exciting); it was what happened in the meeting that showed me the power of this book in your hand.

We didn't have a cover ready to show them yet, and as we pitched the landscape-design aspect and told them they had an opportunity to change the game, we could feel the tension around the new format. But it wasn't until we talked about the 'pay what you want' concept that we could see it was challenging their thinking. At one point, there was discussion between two of the guys,

Scott and Josh, "Hang on a second; the problem is that the barcodes are linked to the price. So you can't just –." Their colleague, Shayne, cut them off. "Guys if we're going to change the game, we're going to have to start thinking differently," he said passionately. They were yet to read one word of this book but in that moment, Shayne summed up its entire purpose.

Less than 24 hours later, they informed us that we'd landed a world-first book deal, which included a full front-of-store stand display in every location, complimentary advertising space on storelight walls, and front counter displays across Australia and New Zealand. Of the 30,000 books that are pitched to LS Travel Retail each year, about 10 per cent of those books are accepted, and only one or two books per year get the in-store prominence we were given.

WHAT IF IT WORKS?

If it works, you'll get to the end of this book having been introduced to a lot of concepts and hopefully having gained some helpful insights from lessons along our journey that will aid you on yours. But I feel like considering all of the above, there may be a question on your mind. What if the horizontal book with no RRP that is sold to fund the future of a movement that has a goal to impact millions of lives doesn't work?

Can I ask you another question? What if it does? Because the answer to that question is that together we'll go on to do something the world hasn't seen before, together we'll go on to change stuff and most importantly, live to see a day where overwhelming statistics like "1 billion people living in extreme poverty" don't exist anymore.

YOU HAVE THE POWER

The world has changed. Thanks to social media and the digital age, we've become more more connected than ever before, each individual has become more powerful than ever before, and in my experience, each of us is more convinced than ever before of our ability and power to leave the world better than we found it. To play a part in this orchestra called life, we have to be willing to be active participants, not passive observers. We must be willing to dive in head-first while our 'next chapter' is still full of unknowns.

I once heard the phrase "life is a book". I love the idea that every single one of us is writing our own individual book. Some books will be published, and some won't be. But that's not important. What is, though, is the realisation that every day you and I write another page, and every major decision we make or significant action we take can start another chapter. Will you be content to settle for a convenient life, or will you pursue something bigger?

If life is a book, then what's your next chapter?

Dream with us. Write with us. Change stuff with us.

1 The World Bank defines 'extreme poverty' as living on less than US\$1.25 per day. While this definition can seem arbitrary, this is an internationally recognised measure of poverty and is a useful starting point in understanding why and how people live this way. At Thankyou, we know that 'extreme poverty' cannot be defined through an economic measurement alone; poverty encompasses a broader set of measures (such as the deprivation of freedoms, agency and basic human rights).

CHAPTER 1.2
The Journey Begins

The Thankyou movement began
with a very personal moment for me.

In 2008, aged 19 and completing my first year of university, my plan was to build a career in property development. I'd been fascinated with real estate since the age of 12 and my late grandfather had been a builder, so maybe it was in my blood. I thought I could see my future clearly. Little did I know that things were about to take a dramatically different turn.

From a young age, I had been aware, like most people, that global poverty was a big issue. We all see the TV commercials, hear the statistics and absorb the dire situations in developing countries around the world through news bulletins.

I was aware. But I had never stopped to consider just *how* enormous the problem was. Because to me, it was a challenge that was 'out there somewhere'. I had sponsored a child through World Vision, which gave me some peace of mind that I'd done my bit for global poverty. I was also in the headspace, as most teenagers are, that I should focus on establishing my career – and later on when I'd made some money, that's when I'd generously give back.

In the course of my studies, I was researching a project online and I came across some facts about the world water crisis. There was one statistic that really grabbed my attention: in 2008, nearly 900 million people across the world still didn't have access to safe water.

This huge figure really struck a chord with me. It made me feel uncomfortable. I grew up in Australia, a lucky country, now home to more than 23 million people. How could it be possible that almost 40 times Australia's population still didn't have safe water?

The enormity of it stayed with me for hours, and then days. But I have to admit, it wasn't the statistic that had messed me up. While 900 million is an absolutely massive, hard-hitting figure, as a statistic alone it was hard to connect to. What I did connect with were the individual stories.

In developed countries, people walk to the tap for an unending supply of fresh, safe water without a second thought. But in poor parts of Africa, Asia and South America, children can walk for half or even a whole day, to and from uncertain water sources. I found this hard to fathom. For some, it's even worse – years later, I was giving a talk at a university and a young man approached me to say that when he was a boy in Africa, his walk for water was a two-day return trip!

As I continued my research, the most confronting part about this issue was the fact that the water these children spent so much time collecting was of dubious quality. Sometimes, instead of sustaining life, it could end up killing. According to the World Health Organisation, 4500 children die *every day* from water-borne disease (2009).

At this point, all I had seen were facts, figures and statistics. But then I asked myself a question that changed everything. It's a question that, if you ask it yourself, has an answer that may influence the decision you make next – and every one after that.

THE QUESTION THAT CHANGED EVERYTHING

The question I asked, as I sat there that day reading these stories, was this: "What if that were me?"

I considered the fact that I have two younger sisters, Jessica and Melissa, and that if our family had been born into the same circumstances as the children in these stories, it might have been *my* job to collect water for them, day in, day out. I pondered that for a moment. Then I wondered how it would feel to discover that the very same water I collected to help my sisters, could actually kill them. With tears streaming down my face I was confronted by the reality that is daily life for many young people in our world.

I was caught a little off guard. What was I meant to do about it? As those minutes at my computer passed, I knew I could no longer ignore the concept of world poverty – and it had been simply a 'concept' to me, until that point. While I knew in reality that it was not a scenario I'd ever have to live out, the fact that people my age and younger, a lot younger, are faced with food and water insecurity each day – *every* day – hit me profoundly.

Something inside me switched. I became very uncomfortable. I was at university working towards a career path that was all about me, yet at the same time, there were other young people stuck in these dire circumstances beyond their control.

I could have shut my laptop and walked away, but there was this part of me that couldn't pretend it didn't happen. I'd seen it and I'd pictured what that life would look like. So now was I supposed to just go on pretending that a problem *that big* didn't even exist? Something about that didn't sit right with me.

Over the coming weeks, I embarked on an interesting personal journey. I began to view things a little differently. One evening, I went for a walk along Docklands in Melbourne where there are rows of amazing apartments stretching into the sky. And there are so many boats – I really love boats.

It had always been my dream to own a big yacht, but on this evening I remember sitting on a bench and looking up at all of this man-made wealth from a completely different perspective. In the past, I was impressed by it. This time, I got my calculator out and started dividing the cost of each apartment by the amount it cost to give someone water.

I had read in my research that it cost somewhere around $20 to give someone ongoing access to safe water (later, we discovered this can range between $5 and $150, depending on location, soil type, type of solution and size of population).

As I did these calculations, I was astounded. I looked down at the marina. If you divide a $3.5 million yacht – something I thought was so cool only a few weeks earlier – by $20, you come to the figure of 175,000. That wasn't just a number. It was 175,000 individuals whose lives could be changed and improved through access to safe water.

I like figures and so you can imagine where my next hour went; adding up and dividing the cost of apartments and boats and going over 'what if' scenarios in my head. This was just one of many experiences that really opened my eyes. I just couldn't get past the idea that the money was *here*, and we just needed to somehow get it *there*. Little did I know how powerful that idea would one day become.

As I continued to research the world water crisis at that time, I discovered something mind-boggling: in Australia, we spent roughly $600 million on bottled water every year. Worldwide, the figure was closer to $50 billion annually. That was in 2008. Since then, the current bottled water industry totals almost $100 billion.

I'm not sure what your view on bottled water is, but I always had (and still have) the opinion that it is a pretty ridiculous product. While in so many parts of the world tap water quality is questionable, leaving bottled water as the only option, Australia's tap water is some of the best in the world and in every city, you can safely drink it without a filter. When you look at the hundreds of millions of people without access to safe water, and then consider the amount of money we Australians spend each year on a product we can actually obtain for free, the absurdity and injustice of it is overwhelming.

But, negatives aside, I saw these two water extremes as a huge opportunity. Yes, we may think bottled water is ridiculous, but we all buy it from time to time because we are thirsty and it's convenient and we don't want a sugar-packed bottle of soft drink. The fact is we're willing to pay for the convenience of bottled water. But, I thought, what if we could turn our love of convenient access to water into safe water access for people in developing countries?

THANKYOU: THE BIG IDEA

An idea was brewing: what if we launched a brand of bottled water to help solve the world water crisis? No doubt, it was a bold idea. I started sharing it with some close friends, who ultimately became our co-founders. They say you probably shouldn't go into partnerships with your best friend or girlfriend. I did both. My best friend Jarryd was in straight away. He'd been hearing me talk and said, "Whatever you need, just let me know and I'll make it happen." I think his first job in the business was 'Head of Documents'. On reflection, I'm not exactly sure what that job title meant, but he had a keen eye for detail and my strength definitely wasn't interpreting documents, so I figured he should be in charge of that. Did I mention we hadn't run a company before?

Jarryd was studying finance and his job in our organisation quickly turned into a finance and operations role. He now manages tens of millions of dollars and all of our product operations as our Commercial Director. Jarryd has more depth and wisdom than most people twice his age. His eye for detail has saved us many times and built Thankyou into an organisation that will hopefully outlast us all. To this day, he still says that same thing when I approach with anything to do with the business: "Whatever you need, just let me know and I'll make it happen."

My girlfriend at the time, Justine, had travelled to developing countries before and had been passionate about business since she was a teenager – she had even won a high school business competition. Her dream was to run a business that existed to help people get out of poverty. You can imagine her reaction when I shared that I was moved by this and had an idea that required business-savvy to execute it. She was in.

Justine was also passionate about marketing and HR. She started out first as our 'Head of Volunteers', because we didn't have staff (and actually, no volunteers at that stage, either). Our team quickly grew to 20 volunteers and as our business expanded and we began employing people, she transitioned into Director of People & Culture. Over our journey, she has driven the growth of one of the most remarkable and inclusive staff cultures you could imagine. At university while studying HR, Justine took some marketing subjects, which quickly turned into a marketing major. So, she went on to also head up our marketing team, leading the implementation of world-first marketing campaigns (you'll read about these soon). It's probably pretty high risk to go into business with your girlfriend, but Justine's last name is now Flynn – we got married in 2010 – so you could say things worked out pretty well between the two of us.

I have another friend, Morgan, who was just one of those kids who is a whiz at everything. He was employed as the operations manager of an entire company when he was only 18! It wasn't long before he was heading up our sales division and using his entrepreneurial skills to help build our business. A little later on in the journey, Morgan kept saying there was this really impressive girl we needed to have on the team. Nicolette joined us shortly thereafter, heading up all of our water projects. Morgan was happy Nicolette joined the team… so happy that he went on to marry her (there was way too much love in the office!).

After investing years of hard work to get Thankyou Water (which later evolved into Thankyou) off the ground, with Morgan driving sales and putting every ounce of energy into getting our water brand stocked in cafés around the country, and Nicolette setting up a world-class giving framework for our organisation, they moved on from the business to chase some other dreams. We're forever grateful for their input and sacrifice in those early years.

There were many more people who sat around in brainstorming meetings and played a huge part in helping us get off the ground. Without this group, who dedicated this stage of their lives to starting our journey, Thankyou would not be here today.

So, what exactly was our initial idea? It was simple. We, as a team, thought we'd take on some of the world's largest multinational water brands and launch our own brand of bottled water. The difference would be that our brand existed 100 per cent to empower Australians to fund life-changing water projects in developing countries. Meaning that after covering all the costs involved in bringing people a great bottled water product, every single cent of profit remaining would be used to fund water projects.

100 PER CENT FOR THE CAUSE

Quite simply, we believed that if we wanted to do something that would truly change the world, then our driving mission had to be one that would genuinely benefit those in need on a lasting basis. Our cause wasn't the afterthought or the marketing strategy – it was the starting point and the entire reason for our business existing in the first place. We now know that what we were starting was a social enterprise.

Names are powerful and our bottle of water obviously needed a brand name. In one of my times of reflection, I remember having a visual picture of a boy drinking water with the phrase 'thankyou' (one word, not two) on the front. I found an image online similar to what I'd imagined and using Microsoft Word, I placed the word 'thankyou' over it.

My first thought was that obviously, you couldn't call a product or a brand 'Thankyou'... Could you? Besides the fact that it's a common phrase, it's not even grammatically correct to spell it as one word. But then I figured a guy called his product Apple (which is a common word) and then another guy called his company Facebook (also not grammatically correct), and both of those brands sort of worked out okay.

People often ask me how on earth we trademarked the word 'Thankyou'. Well, here's the thing – I had a lawyer friend who said that if no one else had done it yet, you could literally put a small TM (which stands for 'trademark') next to a word (to prove you're using the word as a trademark), which would help with eventually applying to officially register it. So that's what we did; we simply wrote TM and stuck it on our bottle label. It wasn't until years later that we finally secured the trademark in the industries we operate in!

We loved this word and were optimistic enough to think it might stick. The word was so simple, yet powerful, and we hoped Thankyou would eventually become more than just a brand of bottled water – that it would evolve into a much larger movement.

We had huge dreams from day one, some of which are unfolding now, but we had to force ourselves back to reality pretty quickly. Because there was one rather large problem in front of us that we didn't know the answer to… How do you even *start* a bottled water company?

It was a very good question because at the time, we had no idea if it was even possible to start a bottled water company from scratch, let alone how to go about it. So we did what any switched-on young person would do: we Googled it. Quite a few results came up, which was helpful. As it turned out, this wasn't the last time we'd consult with our good friend Google.

Over the next few months, we invested countless hours into researching how to get our idea off the ground. We were told we would have to pay to have our own unique bottle created, which after further research, we discovered could cost upwards of $150,000. As if that wasn't a big enough deterrent, we learned that we would also need a minimum $100,000 in cash or finance to cover the first run of product. When we sat back and considered that we were up for over $250,000 in start-up expenses, we thought we might be in slightly over our heads. We still joke that at that time, we probably collectively had a 'combined net worth' (the term rich people use) of about $1000.

"WHERE WILL YOU GET THE START-UP CAPITAL?"

I met up with a couple of business people I'd connected with to share our plans, and they were not as confident as we were about the idea. It was our proposed business model that seemed to be most confounding for people to understand. From the outset, we decided that any profit, even a small amount, would go directly to fund water projects. But these business contacts, as well as many other people that we shared our idea with, expressed the view that this concept was commercially unsustainable and therefore unlikely to work.

People advised us that, as a start-up, we should wait to distribute profits to shareholders (or in our case, our cause) until we were fully sustainable, which would likely be at the three- to five-year mark. While that might give you a round of applause in business circles, to have just broken-even after five years of running your business was unthinkable to us. We knew that selling a product like ours on the promise that we'd fund a project in five years' time was simply not an option. The fact that we existed solely for our cause from the outset meant we needed to give right from the start.

One of the businessmen I met with asked, "But where will you get the start-up capital?" I thought, but didn't actually say, "Well, that's why I'm meeting with you…" The simple solution to his question was to introduce multiple shareholders, but we were adamantly against that, because then the business would exist not only for our cause, but also to financially satisfy our investors. We soon realised that we were at the start of a long journey of being told what "wouldn't be possible".

In retrospect, it's not all that surprising that people didn't have faith in our ability to achieve our goals. We had no business experience, we had no money and we were adamant that we were going to take on the biggest bottled water brands in the country and funnel the surplus profits of the $600 million Australian bottled water industry into helping eradicate the world water crisis. If I had been in their shoes, I may have had the same bemused look on my face as many of them did.

Fortunately, something that has stuck with us from the very beginning is this concept articulated by Muhammad Ali: "Impossibility is not a fact, it's an opinion." We were attempting to change the way things had been done before. We were attempting to go against the way things had always been done before. We were taking on multibillion-dollar businesses with a disruptive 'social enterprise' model that was barely recognised in the business world.

The late Steve Jobs once said: "The people who are crazy enough to think they can change the world are the ones who do". The key word right there is "think". To make your ideas a reality you must have a mindset that actually *believes* something is possible. On paper that might sound easy, but executing that idea can be one of the greatest challenges.

I recently spoke at a conference run by a particularly successful businessman and his introduction caught me off guard. He humbly told the audience that he had met me as a "kid" and had heard me talk about our concept, and back then had thought to himself: "That kid is crazy, that's never going to work". He went on to say how incorrect he was and how it was his honour to introduce me.

The truth is, he was just one of *many* established, successful people who were convinced that our idea would never work. I met millionaires, and even a billionaire, who all advised us not to waste our time. These were smart, well-meaning people, but they didn't buy into our vision or believe that what we believed was possible.

To change anything you must be willing to do things and look at things in a way they have never been looked at before. Your greatest blockage in this regard can actually be your past experience or prejudices. Our lack of industry knowledge and experience coupled with our dream meant that we were wide-eyed enough to see our goal as possible. You may not have experience in whatever it is you are about to change and this could be your greatest asset. Use it to your advantage. You don't know what you don't know, which is often used as a negative connotation, but to me it means you haven't had experiences that could fuel a fear of failure.

If you do have experience, you're about to go on one of the most challenging parts of your journey, because you'll be forced to question everything you've always been taught. To put it bluntly, you have to have a child-like mindset when it comes to your idea. Sometimes I wish we could all be children again. They question everything, they ask "why" and see all things as possible. To really change anything, that's what you need to do. You have to begin to question the way you've always done it, and aim for the 'impossible'.

PARENTS' SUITS AND 'P' PLATE LICENCES

After no luck getting support from established business people, we decided to take matters into our own hands. We thought (and hoped) that maybe we wouldn't need as much start-up capital as we were first advised. We found the details of manufacturers that bottled water for some of the big brands and courageously approached them.

By some miracle, many of them agreed to meet us and I'll never forget those first meetings. My dad generously let me wear his Hugo Boss suit. We always took the 'P' plates (signs you put in your car window in Australia when you first get your driver's licence) off the car as we drove into corporate parking lots – just in case an executive happened to see us in the car park and got clued into our youth and inexperience. We parked my slightly beat up 1995 Ford Falcon and Jarryd's 2001 Holden Commodore next to brand new Porches, Mercedes' and BMWs that filled the car park. Then we walked in confident, ready to pitch our big idea.

In each meeting, we'd open by explaining that we were launching a huge brand of bottled water in Australia. Every manufacturer, including those that bottled for the major brands, was quick to tell us how hard it would be to crack the "saturated" or "flooded" market. While the huge amount of water-related puns made in these meetings was a little amusing, what wasn't all that funny was that they all seemed convinced the market was incredibly difficult to enter, let alone succeed in.

When asked what our unique angle or marketing spin was, we'd confidently say, "Unfortunately, we can't share that with you due to confidentiality. Right now we're here to determine if your bottling plant has the capacity to handle our brand."

With raised eyebrows and hesitant body language, most factories gave us the information we needed. Their trading terms consisted of minimum annual outputs in the millions, to which we confidently rolled our eyes while nodding, as if to say, "We will obviously be selling millions of bottles."

There were a few too many acronyms and other technical details being thrown around by the factories than we were comfortable with. This is how we developed the art of smiling and nodding while madly scribbling notes with words and phrases to type into Google later.

It turns out that the 'smile and nod' can get you through a lot more meetings than you think it can.

As much fun as the first few meetings were, we knew that we had a big problem: we still needed funding. I once read a line in a business book when I was younger. It said something along the lines of, "If the idea is good enough, the money will always come." I couldn't tell you the line before or after that, and I'm sure I took it completely out of context, but I can tell you that I really liked this line. We were convinced that this idea was a winner and the fact that we didn't have the money was just a minor detail.

There was also a defining moment for me in my personal life that changed everything and gave me the confidence for this next stage of the journey. We'll get to what happened later but first, I want to share the details of how we got our 'big break'.

During our meeting with the fifth factory, we dropped the whole "confidential" facade and shared our vision. The manager rocked back in his chair and said, "I've been in this industry for 10 years and I'm with you, I think bottled water is crazy." He went on to agree to bottle our water for us, and then went one step further by offering to defer payment for the cost of goods until we got paid. We couldn't believe it. He was willing to let us have a crack at this idea with no upfront money required. We left the meeting feeling crazily excited, but there were more hurdles ahead, of course. We still needed to find a way to get hold of our own unique bottle shape.

MEETING WITH THE MAJOR PLAYERS

There are two major players in Australia when it comes to packaging, and our next step was to book a meeting with the biggest of them, Visy. We locked in a meeting with the CEO. After sharing that story with a few people, I often got the question, "How on earth did you guys get a meeting with the CEO of one of Australia's largest companies?" It was actually pretty straightforward.

To secure the meeting, I called the main number on the website and asked to speak with the CEO's personal assistant, dropping the CEO's first name in the process. Key lesson: it turns out there is no better strategy than using someone's first name to get straight through the first gatekeeper. I was put through and I explained that I needed to meet with the CEO regarding a proposal. His assistant asked me to put that in an email, which I then did. The email said, "I have a proposal for Mr... and I would like to arrange a meeting." She quickly replied with, "No, you'll need to outline exactly what it is you want to meet about."

We weren't quite sure how to approach this, as we didn't want to share too much too soon and blow our chances of securing a face-to-face meeting. So we reverted to a tried and true strategy and I replied, "Unfortunately, the proposal is confidential and we will only be discussing it in person with Mr..." Shockingly, it worked. An email with a meeting invite arrived shortly thereafter. We were in!

A few weeks later, Morgan, Jarryd and myself were travelling up an elevator – parents' suits back on – to meet the CEO of one of Australia's largest companies. We walked in the door and I'm telling you, it felt like we were characters in a movie as we made our way towards the big corner office.

We had asked for 15 minutes of his time because we thought that was about the limit of how much time we could ask of a very busy executive. We were in and out within about five minutes. I think that may have had something to do with the answer I gave to his question at around the four-minute mark.

He asked a series of questions very quickly and then it came to this one question, which is perhaps, on reflection, a question we should have thought about *before* we went into the meeting… When he asked the question, "So what do you want from us?" I was momentarily lost for words. I'm not sure why we didn't plan an answer to this but for some reason, I had the idea that this was a 'let's figure out how we can support each other' sort of appointment. Keep in mind it was our first major corporate meeting – ever.

I paused for a beat and attempted to look confident. I could sense that this was one of those moments that required direct eye contact and an intelligent reply. Then I said the first thing that rolled off my tongue: "We'd like 10 million bottles per year… for free."

I think you can imagine his facial reaction. My thought process in that split second was that since this *was* a big company, I should propose a big number and hope for the best. It didn't seem to have the effect I had hoped. He was very nice to us but I think he may have had more pressing things on his schedule that day, as we were out of that office about 30 seconds later.

We walked away thinking that given its short length, the meeting hadn't gone well. So we were thrilled when Visy came back with an offer to provide us with a one-off donation of 30,000 bottles, as well as a stock bottle shape that no major groups were using at the time. Now the drop from 10 million bottles annually to a 30,000 bottle, one-off donation does sound big, but when you're starting with a base of 0 bottles and you get 30,000 – well that's a very big number. This was a *huge* win. Up until that point, we had been stumped as to how we could get over the $150,000 investment hurdle to get our own bottle shape, and all of a sudden we had our bottle – for free.

With our bottle mould secured, we headed back to the factory that had agreed to support us. In that meeting, the manager asked us how we were going to launch. He explained, once again, the difficulty we'd have in cracking the bottled water market and how the major multinational players had such a stronghold. Confidently, we told him that those facts didn't worry us because we had a plan. He asked us what exactly that plan was, since he was so generously supporting us. We confidently replied, "We are meeting with a company called MBC (Metro Beverages Company)." He promptly rocked back in his chair and broke out in laughter. We'd obviously missed what was funny about this plan, but he was happy to fill us in.

"Guys, I love your passion, but MBC are the largest private distributor of beverages in Australia," he said. "They only carry the big brands like Lipton Ice Tea and Red Bull. They're not going to look twice at a new operator. Start with a small distributor and work your way up, and maybe in time when you've built a brand, they'll be interested." As we left that meeting I thought, "He's probably right." But another thought followed it immediately: "What if he's wrong?" That second thought has turned out to be the most valuable question we've ever asked and to this day, we continue to ask that question – often to our benefit.

SMILE AND NOD, THEN WORK OUT THE DETAILS LATER...

Our next step was to book in a pitch meeting with MBC. We were successful, but we were told we only had 10 minutes to sell our idea.

Just to give you the full picture, all we took to this meeting was a mock-up A3 poster (created by a friend who happened to be a designer) of what Thankyou Water would look like, because we still didn't have a physical sample product. We were waving our hands around, talking about changing the world when we threw in this bold line: "You have an opportunity to be part of something that is going to change the world or you can sit by and watch someone else, probably your competitor, get on board with us."

We weren't trying to be arrogant; we just really believed in this idea and we were convinced it would work. Our 10-minute meeting allotment turned into over an hour of negotiating; there was a lot of detail discussed back and forth. Near the end of the meeting, one of the directors of the company made a commitment.

"We'll take a first order of 50,000 bottles," he said. "How quickly can you get it to me?" Awkward pause.

Now, keep in mind this was the pitch that wasn't going to work because "you'll never get in". I replied, "Give us three weeks." He looked surprised as he said, "That's pretty quick." I smiled and nodded. We had no idea about manufacturing lead times – to a group of university students, three weeks seemed like a long time. We've since discovered that's *not* the case in manufacturing.

We walked out of the meeting feeling completely ecstatic about what had just happened – but our excitement at landing this first, significant order quickly wore off, when I suddenly had this sinking feeling caused by a huge dose of reality.

You see, before you pitch your Big Idea, you're meant to do a bunch of sensible things like register your company name, organise insurance and ensure your business is legally sound and structured correctly. The list goes on and on and on. We hadn't done *any* of those yet – not because we didn't want to, but because we didn't have any money to do them.

We figured we'd just get out there and get some experience presenting and maybe get some expressions of interest from some distributors, and then deal with the technicalities way, way down the track. Realistically, it's not like anyone was going to order in the first meeting, right?

Wrong.

We now had three weeks to not only deliver real product – which was about to stress our factory manager out in a very big way – but to also make our organisation more legitimate than the A3 poster we had been holding in our hands!

THE IDEA WAS CATCHING

A few days later, I was sitting down for lunch with my business mentor. We'd caught up previously and I had mentioned the Thankyou concept in its very initial stages. When he asked me, "How's the little water idea going?" I replied, "Pretty good actually!" I started to explain that we had a factory lined up, that Visy was on board and we had an order for 50,000 bottles. He nearly fell off his chair.

He then asked where we were getting all our money from. I'm sure I went a little red in the face when I sheepishly replied, "Well, we don't actually have any."

I'm not sure what you're like when it comes to asking people for money. I find it awkward asking to borrow money for lunch, let alone asking for the huge sum I was about to propose to my mentor. We actually only had days to come up with the funds we needed – around $20,000 – to register and set up the company, organise trademarks, arrange various insurances and order our first run of labels – otherwise we were about to mess up our distribution 'deal of a lifetime'.

As carefully as I could, I explained our situation to him. He didn't say too much. He certainly didn't offer up a loan. As we wrapped up lunch I was a little disappointed, as I had hoped he might be the answer to our financial woes. It hadn't eventuated and I was stumped about what to do next.

Thankfully, I didn't have to worry for long. A few hours later, I received a call from him. What he said to me is forever etched into my memory. It turns out that he went back to his office and told his business partner, one of Australia's most successful businessmen in his field of expertise, about our conversation. They were inspired by our story, and impressed that we didn't just have an idea and talk about it, but that we had the guts to back ourselves and attempt to make it a reality. And so, he said, he was prepared to back us too.

"By Wednesday, you'll have a cheque for $20,000," he said. "Go for it."

It wasn't a loan. It wasn't an investment. It was simply a gift. We were speechless. They didn't have any strings or conditions attached to their money. They didn't want control, they didn't want a return – they just wanted to give us a kick-start.

They may have made that decision because they believed in our cause, or in us, but whatever the reason, what they did that day was worth far more than the dollar figure. It's hard to describe the feeling you get when someone with more experience, wisdom and resources than you, believes in you and your idea; it gives you a confidence you never knew you could have.

I don't know if they'll ever fully realise how significant their gift was. We are where we are today because of remarkable people like them.

I have a clear memory of Jarryd and I carrying the cheque to the bank. We couldn't get over the fact that the little piece of paper we held in our hands represented $20,000. It was the largest amount of money we'd ever carried or even physically seen before. We banked the cheque and then registered everything we needed to register, got our labels printed and sorted out a hundred other little things in between.

We set up and registered Thankyou Water Pty Ltd (now Thankyou), our business name, as well as the Thankyou Charitable Trust, which to this day 100 per cent owns the business. This unique structure, with no individual shareholders or personal beneficiaries, means that we can exist for the sole purpose of funding our cause.

The following few weeks were some of the craziest weeks of our lives as we finished off marketing plans, completed our website (with the help of a small army of creative geniuses), designed marketing material and kicked off the process of finding project partners to work with.

The commitment I'd given to our distributor that our product would be on their floors within three weeks wasn't just a huge mission from a manufacturing point of view. It meant we literally had to create a brand overnight. We'd spent months planning and in an ideal world, we should have spent months, not weeks, executing the launch of our product. But it isn't a perfect world, so we had to hustle. I'd like to say that this was the first and only time we jumped in well over our heads before we knew how to swim, but it would turn out to be only the first of many swimming lessons.

SOME THOUGHTS TO TAKE AWAY:

ONE. Let yourself ask questions you don't usually ask. In my case, "What if that story was me?" kicked off our entire journey. Let yourself look at challenges that, in the moment, seem overwhelming and that you feel way too small to take on. Let yourself dream like you were a kid again, when everything seemed possible.

TWO. Don't let your five-year personal or team plan get in the way of an adventure as you work to make your ideas a reality. Your course may be set – in my case, it was my degree in project management – but what about the possibilities that might exist away from the path laid out in front of you?

THREE. "What if it works?" These are four of the most powerful words you can ask. Your experience (or other experienced people) may be quick to write off ideas because they disrupt the status quo. But you can't create something new, you can't change stuff, by filtering every idea through experience. With those four words, you too may find that impossibility is only someone else's opinion and not a fact.

FOUR. Everyone talks about their ideas. Few are bold (or maybe naive) enough to act on them. Some of the best ideas the world has never seen are no doubt stuck in graves because people didn't take the next step. Don't just talk; create action and see who you can inspire along the way to join you.

FIVE. Be way, way more prepared for meetings than we were.

CHAPTER 1.3

Turning Stumbling Blocks Into Stepping Stones

*One thing is certain, for both you and I and
for everyone who will ever dare to turn their ideas into reality.*

We will all face setbacks and stumbling blocks. I believe it is our ability, or lack thereof, to learn from them that will determine whether or not we succeed. In fact, I'd go as far as to define success as the ability to turn stumbling blocks into stepping stones. I like this definition because it removes the illusion of success being achieved when you reach a certain destination. Rather, success becomes about the journey – learning from and overcoming the stumbling blocks we see before us.

At Thankyou, our team lives and breathes by this definition of success. We no longer see problems or even challenges; instead we see stepping stones or opportunities for creative solutions. Where we are today is genuinely a by-product of living this out. You see, changing stuff and turning ideas into reality doesn't come as a result of a series of 'easy wins'. If it did, well, our world would look very different, and you and I certainly wouldn't need to read books like this for inspiration and insight.

As you've read the beginning of our story through the first couple of chapters, you probably thought we had it pretty good. Money dropped into our hands, we got some lucky breaks, and all the right doors opened for us. When it's all packaged up neatly to sit within the pages of a book, it reads like a dream.

But after getting off to a flying start, it wasn't long before we experienced a devastating dose of commercial reality. It was our first stumbling block and unfortunately it was a pretty big one. It began the day that our very first order for 50,000 bottles was dispatched to MBC – the bigwig distributor that had given us the break of a lifetime.

The order was sent directly from our factory to the distributor; but we figured we should also see what the product looked like, so we organised for one pallet to be delivered to my parents' garage (otherwise known as 'our warehouse'). As we unwrapped the pallet, we were beyond excited – this was the moment that we would see our very first run of product in the flesh.

As we opened the boxes, our excitement rapidly faded. The team grew quiet... dead quiet. In horror, we discovered that in every box, the labels on a number of bottles were scrunched; some were crushed so badly that you couldn't even read them. In a state of shock, we sorted through the rest of the pallet. We were stunned when we realised that every single box was the same – meaning roughly a third of all the bottles in our pallet had almost illegible labels.

I called the factory immediately. After a few phone calls back and forth they said, "We're so sorry... The quality control guy was away." I wasn't sure that was even legal. After further investigation we discovered that it wasn't just this one pallet that had been affected, but the *entire* run.

I put a call through to MBC and flagged with them that we would need to get the product withdrawn before it rolled out into stores. As I listened in shock, it was explained to me that it was too late for that – our product had already started going into stores across the country.

This was not a good outcome; it meant that our distributor's staff had to physically pull product back out of stores. It also meant that our inaugural launch was also our inaugural product recall, which we learned could cost thousands of dollars (while the factory covered those costs, we could never recover our lost profits, as we missed out on thousands of sales). It's the type of setback that could easily end a fully established brand – and we had barely even begun!

"THERE'S SOMETHING IN THE WATER"

We got the bottles back, sorted out the labels and re-launched our product about two months later. All's well that end's well, right? Not quite… Another month passed and I found myself in the car driving down the freeway with a bottle of our water on the passenger's seat, my heart racing. We'd received a few calls and emails to say something we never, ever wanted to hear: "There's something in the water."

It makes for a nice song lyric (Brooke Fraser's 'There's Something in the Water' is a great tune) or even a catchy movie title, but it's not a line you want associated with your newly launched bottled water company – especially following a recall.

I'd like to say people were just imagining things. But when we investigated, we could see little particles floating in the water. We'd reported it to the factory but we wanted to know ourselves, via a third-party testing lab, what on earth was going on.

Within a few hours of the test, we got the good news that the particles weren't harmful to humans. We were told it was the result of a potential issue with the lids, and that the same issue had happened to other brands in the past. Further investigation revealed that the fault was not with our factory, but with the lid manufacturer.

We were assured it would never happen again, but at this stage it didn't matter; our reputation was tarnished yet again. Supply is where even the greatest ideas and most innovative brands can quickly fall apart – a lesson we have unfortunately learned time and time again.

Some time later, after recovering from our label recall and water quality mishap, we got a call from the factory to report another problem. They had forgotten to put the neck tags on. The neck tags on our bottles had a big, bold statement declaring "100 per cent of our profits fund water projects". It was our key message and our point of difference, and we really needed it big and bold, so that it stood out to consumers.

It turns out that they had run 20,000-plus bottles without the neck tags – and worse, they didn't have the staff numbers to fix the problem. We immediately called everyone we knew to get them down to the factory for a 'Thankyou Water Fun Day' (aka asking your friends and family to give up eight hours of their time to put neck tags on 20,000 bottles).

Our competitors had the latest, state-of-the-art machinery and processes, and we had our friends and family on the production line. At the time, we were stressed and frustrated, but it's funny how in hindsight moments like these have become some of our favourite memories. In the eyes of optimists (ie our team) our idea was well on its way to success. The realists (ie most other people) would say we were struggling big time to get the idea off the ground.

Until this point, we had been working out of our car boots and our parents' lounge rooms and garages, but the time had come to secure an official space as headquarters for our growing enterprise. We leased what could affectionately be known as a hole-in-the-wall office with zero per cent natural light, from a kind businessman who offered us very cheap rent.

We crammed five desks into that tiny office. It didn't matter about the lack of light, cramped space or the unpleasant smell (due to pretty average ventilation). We were building a world-changing organisation – and we were on our way to big things!

Desk sharing was common and everyone in that little office knew and heard everything that was going on, both business and personal. We loved it and hated it all at the same time. Looking back now, they were pretty special years. We dreamed big and we worked long hours, without ever really knowing if it would pay off.

Still, the most challenging part about working day in and day out on our dream wasn't the working conditions, the small rustic surroundings or the fact that we weren't paying ourselves salaries. It was the fact that we seemed to keep failing.

Six months into selling our water product, now nearly 12 months into the whole journey, we were in roughly 350 independent cafés and outlets. We had hoped it would be in thousands of stores by this stage, but it was surprisingly hard to get people to stock the product. These 350 stores represented our blood, sweat and tears; we'd got them on board through knocking on doors and selling our concept directly to store owners. It was a hard slog.

The market was so price-driven and because there were so many players in the market, the margins were insanely low. We were stunned to discover that most bottles of water, which retailed for $2 to $3 each, were sold to retailers for between $0.30 and $1.00, leaving only cents worth of profit for product manufacturers – ie us!

Alongside the challenges that we faced in the retail market, our factory, which had previously promised us the world, was struggling to keep up with supply. It got to the point where, during one five-week period, our supplier didn't deliver any product at all. It certainly hurt us – big time. In fact, it was the catalyst that managed to lose us about 300 of our 350 customers.

We had also just launched with a new distributor in Queensland, whose response to our lack of supply was, "You're just kids, you don't know what you're doing." You guessed it: they dropped us. This was hard to swallow because while we were young and inexperienced, we weren't the ones running the factory.

As we celebrated our one-year anniversary, as much as I hate to admit it now, we were spent. We were ready to throw it all in.

OUT OF THE BLUE, A MIRACLE ARRIVES

Some people don't believe in miracles. I do. We experienced one not long after the supply crisis. Out of the blue, Jarryd got an email from a prominent Australian bottling plant to say that they had come across our product, they loved our idea and they were very interested in working with us. It couldn't have come at a better time.

I called the number and told the guy I spoke with that we already had a factory (sure it was about to end us, but it was a factory nonetheless). That said, I told him we'd be happy to meet for a chat. A few days later, we met with him. He gave us a remarkable pitch, offering a better price, a better bottle, new state-of-the-art technology that resulted in less impact on the environment – and the best part was that he proved they could keep up reliable supply. We thanked him for his time and kept it professional by saying, "As you know, we already have a factory, but we will be in contact." We thought the best strategy was to act cool and not look too desperate.

After sitting on the decision for one night, we all agreed we couldn't wait any longer. I called our contact to say yes, we'd move to his factory. Unfortunately, the transition from our initial factory to his was messy and we wound up losing about $20,000 in cash and raw materials.

The changeover was particularly hard for me, because I have always had a strong loyalty to people who have partnered with us. We wouldn't have gotten even this far without the support of that first factory, and for that I am so grateful. Walking out didn't feel good, but we had to protect the vision of Thankyou, which at the end of the day was bigger than our team and our personal feelings. All in all, we were relieved to be in a position to launch our product into the market with the support of a more reliable factory.

Thanks to the new factory, we were able to re-launch. (Two years later, their business was bought out by a multinational and we were forced to look for new water suppliers. Mark and Barry, who run the fastest-growing independent bottled water plant in Australia, came to our rescue and helped take Thankyou to the next level. It seems like we always manage to find new water-bottling partners right in the nick of time!)

Throughout the process, our distributor MBC stuck with us, which was in itself a small miracle. By then we'd also signed with a new Sydney distributor that had a huge share of the Sydney market, distributing drinks to 4000 outlets. Our contact confidently told us, "We'll get you into about 2000 stores within a month."

Now, if you get your calculator out and multiply any number by 2000, it's impressive. So we figured we had hit the jackpot and that this was our moment to blow the lid off the Sydney market and watch our business soar. We sent them a truckload of product and patiently waited for the first sales report.

A few weeks later, we received a letter from a legal firm in Sydney that represented our new distributor. It was not good news: they had gone into liquidation. What did that mean, we asked ourselves? We discovered it meant that you didn't get your money back for a very long time, if ever. It didn't look like our 're-re-re-launch' would take off quite the way we'd hoped.

What was keeping us positive at this point was the fact that we had pitched our product to two medium-sized retailers in Australia. If just one of them came on board, it would change everything for our business. We had been speaking with one of the retailers for three months, and the other for nine months.

Unfortunately, these potential deals didn't amount to anything. It was disappointing, to say the least. We felt defeated. It was a little *more* disappointing when, soon thereafter, they both came out with their own brands of bottled water that went towards funding water projects... One of the labels was almost identical to ours, even using similar brand colours.

Don't get me wrong – we were pleased that they were doing something for the cause we were passionate about. However, from a business perspective it was tough to take such a massive setback after 18 months of hitting brick walls.

Knowing that there were bigger retailers in the market, we decided to push on. There are two big players when it comes to Australian supermarkets, and between them, they own 70 per cent of the market: Coles and Woolworths. In January 2009, we presented to one of them. In the first meeting, the buyer said he recognised our passion, but affirmed that we were operating in a tough market and questioned whether we had what it took to compete in the grocery sector.

In truth? He was right. Because we weren't bringing a new innovation to their shelves, they wanted to see some serious marketing investment before they'd agree to stock our product. It's a risk for supermarkets to range a new product, because it often means they have to take another product off the shelf – a product that could be working really well – to make room.

The tough thing for any start-up brand in the fast-moving consumer goods space is that they are up against the major and multinational brands, which have the resources to pump millions of dollars every year into marketing activity. So, telling a retailer that you're building a "grassroots, word-of-mouth movement" using social media and free publicity might get you a smile, but it won't get you a distribution deal.

We remained convinced that our brand awareness strategy would work and ultimately achieve better results than any million-dollar ad campaign, but we also knew that it would take time to prove that point – time that the majority of retailers weren't willing to give us.

Over the next few months, we emailed one of the supermarket buyers regular positive updates. When Katie Holmes came to Australia and was snapped drinking a bottle of Thankyou Water, the photo made it into the Herald Sun online newspaper. You guessed it: this milestone was soon followed by an email to the supermarket buyer from us saying, "See, even Katie Holmes drinks this stuff!"

This particular buyer loved to surf and so it was in our favour that Mick Fanning, the world pro surfer, was a fan of our brand. We had run a marketing campaign, called 'The 400', where we sent water bottles to the 400 most influential people around Australia to ask them to help spread the word about Thankyou. Mick Fanning was one of only a handful of people who got in touch to say he'd be keen to participate.

Jarryd and I met him in Torquay near Bells Beach in Victoria, the mecca of surfing in Australia. As we walked with him through the street and into a café, everyone was staring and you could audibly hear people saying, "There's Mick!" We got to hang out with international surfing royalty for half an hour and afterwards, sharing his support with the supermarket category manager certainly worked in our favour! Cheers for that Mick.

By about September of 2009, we had the guts to tell the supermarket buyer that he was "missing a category on his shelf". It was a big call, considering he was the water expert, and we'd barely been in business two years. "Which category is that?" he asked, to which we replied, "You're missing an emerging category called concept water."

Now, we had made up the name, but we thought it sounded pretty good. We explained that there were two types of water: commodity water and concept water. We pushed the idea that concept water is the future of the water category, because consumers are buying into a vision, not just quenching a thirst. He genuinely liked it and said this 'new category' may have potential.

Finally – the break we'd been waiting for. In January 2010, after 12 months of us going backwards and forwards, I found myself sitting down at this supermarket's head office with this buyer.

After some small talk, he said something I didn't think I was ever going to hear: "Congratulations, you're in – I'm giving you national ranging." I was speechless. We were now almost two years into our journey and after several false starts, *this* was our moment. I'd dreamt of this – it was the tipping point that was going to change everything for us.

While we wouldn't be here without the support of the hundreds of independents and cafés and supermarkets like IGA, Richies, Foodland and countless others who backed our idea, we needed a truly national presence to be a serious contender in the bottled water market. Now, suddenly, we had a national retailer on board – and we were going to be up there with the big brands. Our team, mentors, suppliers, family and friends were celebrating. I can't describe the feeling of landing a deal this big after two years of hard work, overcoming stumbling blocks and setbacks (aka valuable lessons). We'd made it and this was our moment to fly!

A few weeks after that meeting, I called our buyer to confirm the size of the supermarket's first order, so we could ensure that we planned our production runs accordingly. We had learned our lesson from our first massive supply order, and wanted to make sure we could handle the transaction professionally and without any complications.

When the phone was answered, it was a voice I didn't recognise on the other end of the line and I wondered if I'd dialled the wrong number. I asked to speak with our buyer and was told that he had moved to another category. I was stunned. I made a quick call through to the original buyer's mobile phone and he confirmed that he'd been moved, but reassured me not to worry, because the ranging commitment still stood and he'd told the new buyer all about us.

Feeling relieved, I quickly called the new buyer back – but he knew nothing about us. I brought him up to speed about the last 12 months' worth of discussions, gave him the social media, word-of-mouth consumer movement speech and told him that even Katie Holmes drank our water once! Then I reconfirmed the good news that we had a commitment for national ranging. "I'll stop you right there," he said. "I have a new direction for the category. I have the big brands and I have my own brand, and I don't need your water." I protested that we had already received a ranging commitment, to which he said, "That commitment was from an old buyer and it doesn't stand."

End of conversation. End of phone call. End of national distribution deal.

This is the second time in this story where I'll admit to crying (there may or may not have been more). Unfortunately, it wasn't because I'd been moved and challenged by the cruel reality of global poverty. Instead, I felt like someone had just hit me over the head with a bat.

By now, we had been through almost two years of knockbacks as a brand. Added to that, personally, I felt like a complete failure. Leading a team is challenging when things don't go well, and they continue to fail year-on-year. It can take its toll when you're the one assuring everyone not to worry because "once we land this big deal, it will change everything". When that big deal falls over time and time again, you feel like you've let everyone down. On top of that was the frustration that nobody seemed to get our philosophy. All we were trying to do was help people. Why wouldn't anyone catch our vision?!

A NEW DAY, A NEW OPPORTUNITY

As a team motivated and driven by impact, we couldn't throw in the towel just because of a retailer's broken promise. We were extremely discouraged, but there was still a glimmer of hope with another retailer. Yes, yet another one. This was far bigger and really was the deal that would change everything.

Jarryd and I both started our working careers at McDonald's. It's the breeding ground of champions – well at least that's what we like to believe. We both worked at different stores but we had similar jobs, which was unloading stock off the truck. The hardest part wasn't unloading the truck. It was not eating the giant bags of M&M minis and Crunchie bars that go into the McFlurries.

One thing we both noticed was the amount of water unloaded from that truck every Tuesday or Thursday. So naturally, years later, McDonald's was on our hit list of places we needed to approach. As per usual, someone with a lot of experience gave us a 'reality check' that McDonald's never accepted new business; they look to existing suppliers to provide innovation, rather than seeking new relationships. We were well and truly versed with the idea of giving it a go anyway, even if we had just a one per cent chance of success.

A few months earlier, before the supermarket deal fell over, we'd had a weekend that couldn't have gone better if we had tried to script it ourselves. Jarryd, Morgan and I were manning a display stand of Thankyou Water at a conference in Sydney. We were handing out water to passers by and spreading the word about Thankyou, when one of the conference organisers came up to us and said, "You need to go and speak to that guy over there."

Without knowing anything about this particular guy, I walked over to where he was, sat down and introduced myself. I explained our concept and to my great surprise, he said, "I have a client who you should meet – actually, I should introduce you." His client was the CEO of McDonald's.

I was straight on the phone to Justine to share the good news. This is where it gets even better. Two days later, we had a stand at another conference – this time at a coffee trade convention. We were one of 80 exhibitors of products and as we were setting up, we got talking to the guys from the stand next to us. We asked what they did and as the words left their mouths, Jarryd, Morgan and I went as white as a ghost.

They explained their product range and then added, "and we supply McDonald's Australia and New Zealand." Two days, two completely different conferences, but a common theme was emerging.

One of them asked what we did and I delivered the most awkward pitch anyone has ever seen. "That's interesting," he said. "We should introduce you to our colleague when he comes; he manages the McDonald's account." The guy they referred to walked in and this time, I was ready. I told him about our concept. He said, "I love this and I think McDonald's would love it. I'll introduce you to their team." At that point our hearts were racing; I could barely believe what I was hearing.

When someone says, "I'll introduce you", I have learned to have some patience and expect some lead-time before the introduction. So you can imagine my surprise when, two hours later, the guy walked back to our stand with a few people and said, "Hey Daniel, this is the team from McDonald's; you should tell them about your water."

Opportunity doesn't always meet you when you are ready. This was the moment, so I dropped the elevator pitch. They liked it. I continued with the 'walking from the elevator to the office desk' pitch. They still seemed to like it. We loaded them up with as much water as we could physically give them, and the seed was planted.

We got word within 24 hours that they were really excited. My heart is literally racing even as I recount this story, years later. We jumped into action mode as we prepared a formal pitch presentation.

Finally, the day of our meeting arrived. We got off the plane in Sydney and our team was picked up at the airport by our contact. We had brought everyone except Jarryd, who had a prior commitment with the Canadian ski fields. As we signed in as visitors at McDonald's HQ, we were told that they'd received hundreds of pitches for new brands of bottled water and that no one else had even gotten this far along in the process. That took our nerves from about 9 out of 10, to 150 out of 10.

In our preparation, we'd worked out that McDonald's customers could help between 60,000 and 90,000 people every single year. We did a five-year growth projection, which revealed that within a short space of time, they could help over half a million people if they switched to our brand. We presented this projection to five McDonald's executives in their massive boardroom. It went really well and we felt like the pitch was probably the most well received one we'd ever executed. We left feeling pretty pumped about what might happen next.

The following six months were filled with many emails and conversations back and forth between us, our contact and McDonald's. There was a series of hurdles stopping our water from getting in their fridges and we spent months overcoming every single one of them. It was April 2010 when we got the call to say there was just one final hurdle remaining. The market was highly competitive and our pricing had some issues. We worked with all the delivery companies, suppliers and various other parties and submitted a new price. To our relief, we got a response that we'd "removed that barrier". We felt that surely, surely we were close to a deal that could change everything for us…

The next month, May, was a pretty big month. Justine and I had been dating since before we'd founded the organisation and on May 29, 2010, we got married – which was easily one of the best days of my life. We were pretty young to get married but, clearly, we're not the kind of people to allow age to be a determining factor in anything we do. We were both still studying full-time, working nights and weekends to pay the bills and volunteering with the other co-founders around 20–40 hours a week to run our world-changing (or successfully failing) organisation.

While we were eagerly awaiting a call from McDonald's, we were also ready for a break, so we took off for our honeymoon in Bali. Afterwards, we made our way to Cambodia with the team to visit some of the first projects we had funded. It was an incredible, life-changing experience for us all, particularly for me, as this was the first time I had visited the field.

IT'S NOT *JUST* ABOUT THE WATER

While it was clear that our brand wasn't seeing much traction in the market yet, our small successes with independent cafés and other outlets meant that we had been able to fund 50 wells and other safe water solutions in various parts of Cambodia.

In Cambodia, we visited a well-known landmark called the Killing Fields, where we learned more about the country's history and the horrific Pol Pot regime. Pol Pot was a psychopathic dictator. He massacred the people in his country who he felt represented the 'evil' west. Anyone who had a tertiary education, soft hands, wore glasses or believed in any form of religion was on his list. By the end of his reign, he had slaughtered over 1.1 million people.

It's one thing to read about it in history textbooks, but to stand on the fields where so many atrocities took place, actually left us speechless. Understanding the history of Cambodia helps explain why the majority of its people are living in extreme poverty. Even after Pol Pot's reign had ended, and the people began to attempt to re-build their country, most of the people who knew how to do so had been wiped out. I couldn't believe this all happened just 10 years before I was born.

Every knockback, every stumbling block, every disappointment we had experienced on the journey so far paled in comparison to the desperate need we learned of in Cambodia. This trip gave us a whole new perspective, which reinstated the drive to keep pressing on. We saw first-hand that the Cambodian people *needed* others to partner with them. When we visited the communities where we'd already played a part in funding access to safe water, it reinforced our drive and commitment 120 per cent. We had realised that our projects meant people in these communities would no longer be sick with water-borne diseases. But what really moved us was meeting the families and seeing how this access to safe water had completely transformed their lives.

You see, the benefits of safe water access are far-reaching. For example, one family we met was able to save the money they had previously spent on medical expenses to treat water-related illnesses, and instead used that money to buy a motorised plough. That plough was used to tend to the field, grow more produce and increase the family's income. This was just one of many stories that showed us the power of safe water.

Once families have the foundational issue of safe water access sorted, it gives them a real chance at lifting themselves out of poverty. I couldn't help but think that if all our hard work over the first few years had played a small role in partnering with just the few people we had met to see them get out of poverty, then it had all been so worth it!

Sometimes we get caught up in numbers and stats. By financial year one we'd raised $7411 for water projects. By financial year two, we raised $7830 and financial year three saw us raise another $21,000.

By this stage, our third year in, we had funded safe water access for over 2000 people. It was slow progress, but progress nonetheless.

Still, if you do the growth numbers on those three years, it's not overly impressive. We were smart enough to figure out that if we had each worked full-time jobs and each made regular donations to charity, we could have donated more money than our floundering business had generated.

We were stuck thinking that if we were not helping millions of people, then we were not really changing stuff. That perspective well and truly changed on this trip in Cambodia. Prior to our visit, we had thought that because we'd only helped a few thousand people get access to safe water, we had failed. We had forgotten that each number represents an actual person. Every person has value and every person has a story. Even if Thankyou had never scaled as we hoped it would, at that point we knew we had made a lasting impact in these families' lives and that every setback we had faced was worth it.

We came back from that Cambodia trip excited, with a new perspective and more ready than ever to keep building Thankyou; nothing was going to stop us.

THE SIGNIFICANCE OF A PHONE CALL

After a long flight home, I received two phone calls soon after we touched down in Melbourne.

The timing was amazing because I had been away for over three weeks and both calls came in within a few hours of each other on the day we landed.

Let me tell you about our second phone call first; it was from our key contact who had introduced us to McDonald's. He uttered those painful but all-too-familiar words: "McDonald's will not be going with Thankyou Water."

It's safe to say that at this point in our journey, this was my least-favourite sentence. It turns out another beverage company – a multimillion-dollar multinational – had managed to bump us out.

After two and a half years of hearing similar responses, and in this particular instance, several months of prolonged, positive negotiations, this was a devastating phone call to receive. It was also a harsh commercial reality – at the end of the day, it was just our water versus another water.

The team at McDonald's are a great bunch of people who are driven towards innovation and changing the fast food game. But at the end of the day, their hands were tied. When a multinational brand comes in with a deal that seems to make more commercial sense on paper, there's not much that a buyer or even a senior executive can do.

Now maybe this is too bold a dream, considering we are competing with the biggest multinational beverage companies in the world, but I still want to see our water brand stocked in McDonald's Australia. Why? Because if McDonald's Australia had accepted our water in 2010, then in 2016 at the printing of this book, over half a million people would have sustainable access to safe water. And every subsequent five years, another 500,000 people would gain access. I've learned that in 'big business' it always "comes down to the numbers", I don't think we can afford to ever give up on this partnership opportunity.

Will McDonald's ever drop the globally dominating beverage brands for a water product like Thankyou? I hope so. Maybe I'm a little biased about what could happen in Chapter Two of Thankyou's journey, but it's exciting to consider the possibilities.

However, after McDonald's turned us down, we were well over two and a half years into our journey and the knockbacks had come thick and fast. I can understand if you're thinking this is the most depressing start-up story you've ever read.

But wait – let me now tell you about that *first* phone call I received that day. While we had been investing hours upon hours into the McDonald's negotiations, we had also been working on another fairly large deal, with Australia Post. The first call I received that day after stepping off the plane had been from Australia Post to say, "Congratulations, we've approved you for a trial in 20 stores." You may think that compared to national ranging in McDonald's, a 20-store trial is a small deal. But let me explain the significance of that phone call…

Australia Post has the largest retail footprint of any retailer in Australia. When I discovered this, I sent a letter to the CEO as it was too good an opportunity not to chase. But there was one tiny obstacle. In its 200-year history of retailing in Australia, they had *never* had a consumable product for sale in any of their corporate stores. Not one.

After pitching to their CEO in a brief, intentionally vague and "highly confidential" letter, I got a call from a member of his team. This guy asked me what we wanted to meet about; I responded that it was confidential and therefore I would like to speak in person with him. Well, this time that previously tried and true tactic didn't work. He clearly wasn't impressed with my approach so I went on to quickly explain our concept before he hung up the phone.

"I'm glad you explained what you do because it saves us meeting," he said. "In our 200-year history, we've never had a consumable product in our corporate stores and we have a written policy that 'if it goes in your mouth, it doesn't go in our store'." Attempting to think clearly on my feet, I quickly replied, "That's good then, because we are not selling a bottle of water."

"I thought you said you were a bottled water company?" he replied. "No, we are giving your customers an opportunity to change the world and the bottle, really, that's just a little gift we give them to say thank you," I said hastily. The phone went silent – and then he laughed. Next, he asked a very direct question. "Do you mind me asking how old you are?"

I knew this was not a good sign. When I responded that I was 20 (at the time), he went on to say that he loved my passion and that he'd be willing to give me 15 minutes to just have a chat about it. He stressed that Australia Post couldn't do anything due to the policy, but perhaps he could help give some advice.

Since my contact had stressed the point that Australia Post couldn't and wouldn't stock our water, I remember going to the meeting a little under-prepared. We knew we were going up against a brick wall, so Justine and I threw together a thin proposal. We met with our contact and while he admitted he loved the concept, he reiterated again that there was nothing Australia Post could do to help. A few months later, we got a call to say that there was some renewed interest in the product as they were reviewing their retail strategy. After several follow-up meetings, that phone call came through the day I landed in from Cambodia to say that our product had been approved for a trial. If the trial was successful, then our water would be ranged in over 800 stores.

We knew that the big players in the beverage industry had been trying to make this deal happen for decades and somehow, our little brand had made it through the door. The CEO and the wider business team must have seen the potential of our brand – they saw that they would not just be selling a great product, but they could empower Australians to change the world.

So there we had it: a 20-store trial with Australia Post. Finally, after more setbacks than I could possibly list here, a major retailer had come on board, and there was a glimmer of light at the end of what had been a very long, dark tunnel.

SOME THOUGHTS TO TAKE AWAY:

ONE. Every stumbling block we've ever faced has taught us something that ultimately made us wiser, because we forced ourselves to find the learning curve. Every time you fail, ask why. Then ask yourself: "What can I learn from this?"

TWO. I'm not sure about you, but I feel like a pretty ordinary person; so does every member of our team. But what we are attempting to achieve is extraordinary. If you are in that same place, cling on to the wise words of C.S Lewis, who said, "Hardships often prepare ordinary people for an extraordinary destiny."

THREE. Just because you fail again and again, it doesn't mean one day you won't succeed.

FOUR. Sometimes the smallest steps can have the greatest significance. Our 20-store trial with Australia Post might not have looked like much, but it was breaking a 200-year tradition. It's the small steps that can add up to a big change.

FIVE. Just saying something is "confidential" doesn't always land you a face-to-face meeting, but sometimes it does!

CHAPTER 1.4
The 'Why' Behind What You Do

I felt like giving up almost every week.

When I was growing up, I used to have these toys; I think they were called bobo dolls. They weren't really dolls, but a plastic or metallic figure with a rounded base that was weighted at the bottom. What made them so much fun was that it didn't matter how many times you knocked them over, or how hard you pushed them, they always rebounded to standing position.

When you set out to chase your dreams and change anything, the mere chance that your idea could work is enough to drive you. But when the going gets tough and the romance of the idea wears off, you'll quickly find out if you have the internal drive required to get back up each time you encounter challenges.

So far in this story, I've discussed some of the early setbacks we experienced. There were many other bumps in the road that I haven't mentioned, but by now you're probably wondering, "What the heck kept you going?" It's a question I'm often asked; it's either that or, "Did you ever feel like giving up?"

My response to the second question sometimes shocks people – because honestly? The answer is regularly. Jarryd and Justine were the same, and I'm sure many of our team felt like packing it in from time to time, too.

After so many setbacks and challenges and outright failures, it becomes difficult to keep plugging away at your goals. That's where the answer to the first question comes in: I believe the only thing that truly kept me going was my connection to my 'why' – my deeply personal motivation that got me out of bed on those mornings when all I wanted to do was curl up and hide from building this dream, which at times seemed so impossible.

My 'why' kept me going as I worked night shifts as a roadside traffic controller (the people that hold the 'Stop' and 'Slow' lollypop signs), in call centres and in mobile phone shops, earning enough money so I could pay my bills and work the next day at Thankyou for no income while building the dream.

It picked me up after every dead-end phone call, every setback, every knockdown and through many, many moments where I said to myself, "That's it, I'm giving up and walking away. This is just too hard."

Like the bobo doll was weighted to enable it to bounce back up, understanding my 'why' is what weighted me and enabled me to rise after every fall. I'm not saying it was easy, but it gave me strength to keep going.

During the tough times, it can be difficult to see others succeed while you fail. In my case, I was seeing friends graduate from university after I'd dropped out to focus on building a dream (one that, so far, wasn't working). But there are two moments that changed everything for me. They connected me so profoundly to my 'why' that deep down, I knew I would never give up until every last avenue had been explored, maybe even two or three times.

The first was the moment I shared at the start of this book, when I sat in front of my computer and the enormity of global poverty truly hit me. What was powerful about this moment was that it made me uncomfortable enough to get up and do something. The fact that I can now wake up and take action towards helping a cause I'm passionate about – and see it impact not just my life, but the lives of others – is powerfully motivating. This is the 'why' that joins us corporately as a team at Thankyou. We come from many different backgrounds, with many different beliefs and views on the world but the common denominator we share is our passion to eradicate global poverty.

A few months into our journey, the second moment that changed everything for me occurred. It was very personal and felt like it was straight out of a Hollywood movie. I'm not sure if you've seen the movie *Bruce Almighty*, but there is a scene where Jim Carrey is driving down a bridge yelling to Morgan Freeman, "God, if you're real give me a sign." He then drives past a truck full of signs saying 'Wrong Way', 'Stop' and 'Turn Back', before driving past a big billboard that says 'Bridge Closed'. He keeps driving anyway and crashes his car.

Well, you could say I had a moment similar to that. A key driving factor for me is my personal faith. I believe in God and for me, my faith is more than just a nice Christmas or Easter story about Jesus or a set of morals I live by. My faith runs deep and is a part of my day-to-day life. From my personal faith perspective, this idea, Thankyou, seemed perfect – it was such a simple yet powerful way to genuinely help others in a lasting way. But after months of research and meetings that went nowhere, I felt like I'd wasted so much time and it all just seemed too far-fetched and unreachable.

So, back to my movie moment. One day, before we'd even got our first factory on board, I was sitting down and I felt ready to throw it all in. We'd already experienced so many setbacks and I felt exhausted by the impossibility of the task in front of us. I said, "God, if I am meant to do this, then you have to give me a sign. Can you write on the wall, 'Hey Daniel, do the water thing,' or something like that?" It was a long shot, but I was going for it!

This is when it gets a little crazy. After saying that, I picked up the Bible, which was written thousands of years ago, and I opened it. Without flipping the pages either way, I looked down and I read a passage I had never read before in a book called Isaiah. It said, word for word: "The poor and needy search for water yet find none, their tongues are parched with thirst but I the Lord God have heard their cry."

I froze. My heart felt like it was pumping so hard it might burst out of my chest. The passage goes on to say that God will turn the desert into springs and valleys into pools of water. I couldn't believe it. It's one of the only verses in the whole bible that makes any reference to water in this way.

I had just asked for some sort of divine sign, and bam – I got it! I was speechless. This moment changed everything for me personally and gave me a newfound confidence that I was on the right path. You could call this a coincidence; you could say I just have blind faith. But I know this moment was real – and really hard to ignore or disregard, even though there were times when I was tempted to.

These two moments really connected me to my personal drive, my sense of 'why'. And because I know my 'why', it doesn't matter how many times I'm knocked down; just like the bobo doll that has a weighted foundation, I'm able to bounce back again and move closer towards my dream. I share my personal 'why' with you, knowing that yours probably looks completely different. Some of you may even feel like putting this book down because you're saying to yourself, "Did he really just collectively reference God, Jesus and Morgan Freeman?" But my point here is that each person has some kind of 'why' that keeps them going, and it's deeply personal. Motivating forces will be different for every single person reading this, what is important is that you dig deep to find them.

What are the moments that have defined your 'why'? Hold on to them tightly as they will become the positive thoughts that carry you through the dark times.

KEEPING THE FIRE BURNING

Two truths that can seem quite depressing at first glance: success isn't guaranteed, and failure, to some degree, will definitely be part of your journey. In the face of these facts, it can be challenging to keep your passion alive, especially when you face ongoing setbacks and challenges as you strive towards launching your idea.

I have stressed the importance of finding your 'why' but unfortunately, it doesn't stop there. You must also find a way to maintain the passion and burn for your 'why'. It must be your constant companion. Great intentions simply aren't enough to carry you through. I guarantee you, I would not be here writing this if all I had to draw upon were those two defining moments, as amazing as they were. Throughout our journey, I've had to refresh my personal motivation time and time again.

This happened on a recent trip to Africa with one of our project partners. I met Vianney, a 15-year-old boy, in a country called Burundi. We had travelled for a few hours through the hilly regions of a country that most people haven't heard of. It's right next to Kenya and is the fifth-poorest country in the world. I started talking, through a translator, with Vianney and he began to share about what his life was like before he had access to safe water.

You could argue that it was simply another story, similar to others we'd heard many times before, but I can't explain the profound experience of hearing it first-hand from the person who'd actually been through it.

Previously, Vianney would embark on a long walk twice a day to collect water for his mum and grandma. He talked about his constant sore neck and back from carrying 15 litres of water on his head every day. He told us how he had tried carrying smaller containers but it meant he had to walk four times, which he hated. He mentioned how hard it was to believe now, still, that just metres from his front door, he and his family have access to safe water through a gravity-fed water system that taps into natural spring water in the mountains.

I asked if I could go for the walk with him to see where he used to collect water. As we walked down the steep terrain to the bottom of the valley, we arrived at a small, filthy creek. It wasn't water as we would picture it – it was essentially muddy water. He showed us how he used to collect it and then I asked if I could carry it back.

At first, he was confused. Why would I want to carry it back? The translator helped convince Vianney that I wanted to do it, as it dawned on him that I wanted to put myself through the same experiences and emotions that he used to feel every day as he collected water.

We were filming this whole story for a segment on Channel 7's morning television show *Sunrise*, which would give Australia an update on Thankyou, and I knew this would help to visually tell the story. But this small journey carrying water meant so much more to me than that. I wanted to feel the pain and experience, just for a moment, what Vianney had endured every single day for so many years.

When I was back home in the comfort of my office and life in Melbourne, feeling sorry for myself and tempted to throw in the towel because it was all too hard, this was the moment I wanted to draw strength from.

After the walk back up the mountain, my neck was sore and I was exhausted. We sat down and talked some more and then he took great pride in showing our team how his new safe water source worked, which we had played a part in funding. Vianney finished our conversation by saying that when he saw our trucks approaching, "He wanted to lift them up above his head, just to show his appreciation, but he couldn't because he was just a kid." As the translator interpreted his words and shared Vianney's sentiments with us, it was hard to stop the tears from building!

In 2008, in front of my computer, a single moment inspired me to do something about the world water crisis. As I stood next to Vianney five years later, the reason why I do what I do was reinforced to me very powerfully.

Visiting the communities we have worked in with our project partners always reminds us of our 'why', and keeps the fire burning. Not only do these communities now have access to safe water, but so many of the accompanying difficulties these people face without safe water have been eliminated. Women and children no longer face the same dangers of rape and kidnapping on the perilous journey to collect water. People don't have to fear being attacked by wild animals at the waterholes. Hope is restored that they won't be stuck in poverty forever or even face death from water-borne disease.

We are driven by our 'why', our motivation to be part of ending extreme poverty.

Recently, I was talking at a corporate event and one of the board members of the company asked me after my keynote speech, why I was still the managing director at Thankyou. I was a little confused and laughed awkwardly, until I realised it was a real question. He told me that I should let someone else run this little project so I could go off and actually make some real money. "You do realise you won't make any money doing this charitable thing? You need to use your skills elsewhere to make money!" he said. This was a blunt version of a message I've heard many times over.

The question assumes that I've already done a good thing and surely, I'm not planning to spend my entire life pursuing this little charity hobby? In response, I politely smiled and said, "I'm in this for the long haul." But there is a small part of me – the socially inappropriate part, perhaps – that just wants to say, "Did you not hear me? People are dying of preventable water-borne diseases and we are sitting here at this fancy little event, sipping our fancy little drinks and you want to convince me to get a better-paying job?!" As I said, socially inappropriate…

The truth is, I have no issue with fancy drinks at fancy events or people looking for better-paying jobs. My point in sharing the above story is that we each see situations and filter the choices we, and others, make differently, based on our 'why'. And thanks to my 'why', I'm in this for the long haul.

DISCOVERING YOUR OWN PERSONAL 'WHY'

At this point, you're in one of two camps: you either know your 'why' and are able to articulate it easily, or you're wondering if you even have a 'why', and if so, what it is. Where you find your 'why' will be something that only you can discover. But I can give you some thoughts on where to look and encourage you to be open to go on the journey of discovery.

People are moved and motivated to do many different things. I've talked about being motivated by the global poverty cause in my story. Your journey may be (is likely to be) about something completely different. But regardless of what you do, it's impossible to consistently get up and keep going in the face of ongoing challenges, without knowing your deeper 'why'.

As an example, the best teachers are not the ones who turn up to school for a pay cheque – in fact, those teachers are the ones that are often never remembered (neither is their content). My mum is a teacher and I wish I could have had her as my teacher at school! I hear her talk at home with eyes gleaming about what she's hoping to impart into her primary school students, some as young as five and six. She works crazy hours, not the bare minimum.

Now, you might say she's just a teacher, which is kind of just existing in a career – but I know it's far from that. I don't know about you, but I still remember the teachers who made the biggest impact on my life. I remember their names, their faces and what they said. I remember that they believed in me. I remember the lunchtimes they gave up, the after-school input they invested. I saw their passion come out because they were driven to inspire the next generation.

They didn't just teach from a textbook – they had stories, analogies and crazy unconventional ways of teaching. They were willing to step outside of the way things were always done and it woke something up inside of their students.

You may have loved, hated or fallen asleep in the movie *Dead Poets Society* but I loved seeing Robin Williams' character challenge the status quo and inspire his students to "carpe diem" – seize the day. He lost his job for it, but (spoiler alert!) the movie ends with a scene where students are standing on their desks in defiance to the school, saluting their teacher and saying, "Oh captain, my captain."

Robin's character made his students feel something. In a similar vein, game changers evoke feeling because they exist for a purpose. This isn't just applicable to an individual. It is essential that every organisation, whether driven by a social cause or not, is connected to their purpose. Zappos, the online retail giant based in the United States, is a great example of this.

They are a very different business to us. They are disruptors in the online retail space. They grew from the seed of an idea to $1 billion revenue in their first 10 years, and in 2012, they were named number 11 in *Fortune* magazine's list of 100 Best Companies To Work For.

Zappos was actually on the brink of failure when they were forced to discover their 'why': to deliver happiness. From that point on, they made decisions based on their 'why', which sometimes made no apparent financial sense. Case in point: they run a 24-hour warehouse, not for efficiency, but for customer experience. Their KPI measurements across multiple departments are not just time or financially focused, but are based on delivering happiness to the customer. Zappos have been incredibly successful in the commercial sense of the word, and in large part it's because they are committed to focusing on their 'why'.

Whether your 'why' appears to be big or small, every 'why' is significant because it links you to your purpose and meaning in life.

SACRIFICE – OR STRETCHING BEYOND THE COMFORTABLE

Sacrifice is the part of the picture that people often forget to mention when sharing how they turned their idea or dream into a reality. While it's not easy to make, sacrifice is easier when you know your 'why'.

Sacrifice is also the part that you don't always consider when you start building an idea and chasing your dreams, because you're so focused on your end goal that any perceived sacrifices seem completely worthwhile. And they are, but they also stretch us beyond what's comfortable.

When we started Thankyou, we figured, quite naively, that it would take around three months for our social enterprise to start growing. By six months, we thought we would all be able to quit our jobs so we could invest all of our energy and attention into building the brand. If you had told us otherwise, we would have smiled politely and thought, "Well, you clearly don't understand how good our idea is, because this is gonna be HUGE!"

After six months, we weren't earning wages from Thankyou. We weren't even anywhere close to making a living from the business. Knockback after knockback, month after month, we realised that to get our idea to really fly, we had to put more time and more focus into Thankyou. This was tough because we already felt like we were giving it our all.

Jarryd, Justine and I had so many random part-time jobs during our start-up journey. We worked at call centres, in retail, traffic control, nannying and even sorting mail in mailrooms at 4am. I must say that traffic control was one of my favourites. Jarryd and I did it together – we were at opposite ends of roadwork sites, holding the 'Slow' and 'Stop' signs. We managed to get the night shifts, which allowed us to work during the day at Thankyou.

I jumped from job to job, doing whatever work I could that would allow me to maximise my time at Thankyou. One time, we scheduled a particular meeting with Australia Post in the city at around lunchtime. It was a sign-off meeting with the potential to result in hundreds of thousands of unit sales, which meant it was a huge deal and therefore, a full suit occasion.

I left that meeting and drove straight to a house in the suburbs, got changed out of my suit and put some painting clothes on. At 2pm, I started painting the fence at that particular house for some extra cash so we could make rent that week. I remember thinking it would have been pretty funny if one of the Australia Post executives happened to drive past in their car and saw me.

This little story is just one of many that illustrate how much effort and time we invested to make Thankyou a reality. We did whatever work we could find that would give us flexibility to be able to put 20 to 40-plus hours per week into building our dream. The long days when I worked two jobs while also studying were the toughest. While we might have missed out on a lot of stuff that normal young people do, we were willing to make those sacrifices because we were driven to build this dream.

I thought we'd been making enough sacrifices, but another turning point came about when I had been studying for three years, around two and a half years into Thankyou's journey. I realised that I had two choices – to either give it our all, or risk the chance of never getting it off the ground at all. I obviously opted for the first choice, and at the time I knew that if we were going to make this work, I had to defer my university course.

When I dropped out of university, many people thought I was crazy, as I had only one year left. They had a great point: if Thankyou didn't take off, then I didn't have a fall-back and I was just 12 months from attaining formal qualifications. I've since learned that sometimes, having no fall-back is all the more motivation to truly invest your all. At this time, Justine and I were about to get married and both of us only had part-time jobs and no plan B in the pipeline, in the event that Thankyou failed to succeed. This is when we realised that to build this dream it was going to take a lot of personal sacrifice.

Was it worth it? Of course. Was it scary? Definitely. But my 'why' carried me through. In our first year of marriage, there were so many weeks where Justine and I wondered how the bills would get paid or how we'd eat until our next pay came through. Justine, Jarryd and I put it all on the line and in hindsight, it was the best thing we could have done.

It took us three years before we could start paying ourselves base salaries at Thankyou. Even once the salaries kicked in, the reality was that we could have been making more money if we were packing shelves at the supermarket. But even though the pay cheque was modest, it meant that we could finally stop working the second and third jobs and give up the crazy hours, to focus solely on building Thankyou.

Over time, the sacrifices haven't lessened as we may have expected; rather, they've changed. While we'll never (hopefully) have to go back to the days of working multiple jobs to make ends meet, our responsibilities as directors grew (and continue to grow) as the business expands. With great responsibility, also comes great sacrifice.

In business, there is a concept known as risk and return. It essentially means that people are prepared to take a risk if there is a reasonable return on the line. We are young and passionate and our 'return' (other than the salary based on the charitable sector we are paid to do our job, which we could earn anywhere without taking the risks we take) is helping impact people's lives.

I mention the fact that we are young because I recently met a much older, more seasoned social entrepreneur, whose enterprise runs on a 100 per cent model like ours. He's given the past 25 years of his life towards building a globally successful social enterprise. His work has made a phenomenal impact but he was incredibly honest with me about his personal sacrifice. He said, "Daniel, when you're my age and you've built something of significant commercial size, as have your other business colleagues, and they have a lot to show personally for it and you don't have anything other than the satisfaction, it can be hard."

This man wasn't selfish and he certainly wasn't regretting his decision to put his talents and abilities into changing lives around the world, but he was honest enough to say that sometimes, the sacrifices are hard to bear. These are the sacrifices I'm talking about. It's not necessarily a bad thing and it's not something we need to have a pity party over, but it is real.

Your sacrifices may look entirely different to ours, but they will still exist. In your own journey as you make your ideas a reality, you'll have to make many sacrifices (if you haven't already). I share these personal experiences with you to help prepare you for the sacrifices you'll surely have to make.

If I could go back and change anything, including any moment of sacrifice, I wouldn't. It's built the character we've needed in order to go where I know we're meant to go. In my view, the impact we've been able to make far outweighs any sacrifices made along the way.

SACRIFICE, NOT COMPROMISE: THERE'S A DIFFERENCE

I believe it's never too early or too late to find your 'why'. And I know you'll find it, if you just let yourself look hard enough. Along with knowing your 'why', you also need to understand your values or your personal moral compass, to know when sacrifice will compromise something even more valuable than the work you set out to achieve.

In the lead up to Justine and I having our first baby, I was overwhelmed by the number of men – particularly older men – in business, some who I knew well and others who I was meeting for the first time, who opened up about their life as a father. Many had a look of deep regret in their eyes as they started their advice... "If I could just go back again..." they'd say.

Their advice always ran along a similar theme: don't neglect time with your family, no matter how important you think your work is. I am grateful for their warning. I suppose this is an example of sacrifice crossing over into compromise. Sometimes, it's hard to know the difference between them. This is the hard stuff and even as I write this, I'm making a commitment to myself to heed this advice. It's written in a book now, so I'm going to look a little silly if I mess this up. No doubt I won't be perfect, but many have made me aware of the underlying principle that sacrifice can turn into compromise, which is a mistake I'm committed to avoiding and I believe we all need to be, too.

SOME THOUGHTS TO TAKE AWAY:

ONE. A deep connection to your 'why', your purpose, will ground you and give you what you need to make your dreams and ideas a reality.

TWO. To discover your 'why', ask yourself these questions. Find the common denominators in the answers and you'll have your first lead to explore in finding your 'why':

– If money and time weren't limiting factors, what would you allow yourself to dream of doing?

    – What makes you feel angry or rise up at the injustice you see?

        – What gets your emotions going?

          – What brings tears to your eyes?

            – What makes you happy?

THREE. Once you understand your 'why', ensure you find a way to keep the fire burning. Sacrifice is inevitable, embrace it and let it build your character but don't let it compromise your own set of values.

FOUR. Morgan Freeman did a pretty good job at playing God in *Bruce Almighty*.

CHAPTER 1.5

High-Five The Status Quo In The Face – With A Chair

This chapter begins with a fiercely passionate title, for two reasons.

Firstly, the line "high-five the status quo in the face – with a chair" creates a powerful visual. Secondly, and more importantly, it is memorable – and my hope is that this phrase will stick with you long after you've finished this book. From a very young age, we learn how things should and shouldn't be done and we are largely conditioned to follow these rules. But whether we know it or not, simply accepting the status quo can hinder our success.

In the retail space where we operate, the standard process goes something like this: make a product, book a meeting with a retailer and present your product and marketing plan. Then hopefully, if your pitch is good enough, the retailer will give you a shot. After that, your product is rolled out into stores and you press on with an expensive and impressive marketing campaign.

If lots of people buy your product, well, the rest is history. If they don't – your money is spent and the game is over. It's generally smooth sailing for established product ranges that have a proven track record, strong brand recognition and big marketing budgets. But for a cash-strapped start-up? Not so much.

Throughout the first few years of our journey with Thankyou, we met with countless retailers to pitch our idea and discovered a common topic of conversation in these meetings: brand awareness. We were really lacking in this area, and we felt the main reason was because the public couldn't buy our product from a wide range of outlets. But retailers wouldn't stock us until we had brand awareness, so it was a continuing 'chicken before the egg or egg before the chicken' conundrum.

WATCHING THE SUNRISE

A few weeks after returning from Cambodia, I was driving to work and feeling incredibly frustrated. "Why isn't the media supporting us?!" I asked myself. "We're trying to help solve global poverty – the public need to hear about it!"

When I arrived at the office, I sat down and wrote a letter to the then-executive producer of *Sunrise*, the number one-rated morning program in Australia. Now, let's be honest – someone in his position gets hundreds of letters and emails on a daily basis, so realistically I knew the chance of him ever reading my note (let alone responding) was low. But I have never been one to let the apparent impossibility of a situation or desired outcome stop me. So I sent off the letter and two days later, his personal assistant called me and asked if I was available for them to fly me up to Sydney for a meeting later that week.

"Would you be okay with that?" she asked. You could have picked my jaw up from the floor!
"Yes, that should be fine," I replied as calmly as possible.

A few days later, I found myself walking nervously into the Channel 7 studios in Sydney. As I approached the corner office, the producer jumped up to shake my hand and said it was a pleasure to meet me, before inviting someone else to come and join us.

A reporter with the program walked into the room. "I flew Nuala up from Melbourne this morning for this meeting as well," he said by way of introduction. Now, I'm sure she was going to do other things in Sydney that day, but I was impressed that she was in town partly for our meeting. Sitting nervously in my chair, I started sharing our journey. At some point in the middle of the story, he looked me in the eye and asked me a direct question.

"So, is this for real? How does it all work – do you guys make big salaries?"

I explained our social enterprise model, and that it was legally set up so that we could exist 100 per cent to fund life-changing projects. I shared that our long-term goal was to build it to a sustainable point where we could pay staff and ourselves salaries, but that for our entire three-year journey to date, we'd volunteered our time to build the organisation.

I told them how we all worked nights and weekends to earn money to get by, so that we could focus on building our organisation during the week. He was blown away by our commitment to the cause and then asked if he could pitch an idea to me.

"We want to fly you and another team member over to Cambodia and film all the projects you're working on. Then we want to film the factory, distributors and cafés that stock your water, to create a two-day feature for *Sunrise*. Are you up for that?"

I was obviously overwhelmed and as a result, my memory of the rest of that meeting is pretty blurry, but I'm fairly sure I blurted out "Yes!" When our meeting finished, we walked straight into a planning session with one of the show's other producers, and over the next hour we mapped out the story.

Once the planning was done, I called our team back in Melbourne. After three years of delivering disappointing news, this was an amazing phone call to make.

Within a few weeks, Justine and I found ourselves in the Qantas lounge sitting with the producer and the nicest camera crew we'd ever met. This was my first Qantas lounge experience. I certainly made the most of it and stocked up on all the free food.

We filmed for two days on the ground and captured some incredible stories with people we'd been helping, showcasing the water projects that Australians had funded through buying our water. It was a whirlwind tour but thankfully, because we had just been in Cambodia, we were able to revisit some of the same people we'd already met and invite them to share their stories.

There was one moment on this trip that really drove home the significance of what we do. There's a photo at the end of this book of a lady we interviewed, who showed us the water she used to drink before she'd received a Thankyou-funded filter. They say a picture tells a thousand words, but I reckon this picture tells about fifty thousand.

After two full days of filming in Cambodia, we then spent two days days back in Australia filming our factory, cafés and distributors. I figured that because so much filming went into this, it was going to be a huge story, so I was a little disappointed when they said we'd get between three and four minutes of air time over two days. Apparently that was how television worked and we were told we were lucky to receive even that amount of time.

The morning the segment went to air, our team were scattered around Melbourne. Justine was rostered on to nanny before work, which involved taking the kids to kindergarten, so on the way she stopped at a McDonald's and asked them to change the channel so she could see the segment. Jarryd, myself and the rest of the team were at our respective homes and let me tell you, it felt strange watching ourselves on TV. A short while into the story, I checked my watch and realised the segment had gone over four minutes; the story just kept going and ended up being around seven minutes long! Best of all, this was just day one – there would be a follow-up story the next day. I have a clear memory of jumping around our lounge room!

THE IMPACT OF A LITTLE TV LOVE

What followed was insane. After our TV debut, our Facebook page exploded with interaction from the public and our website crashed. Our 1300 number received hundreds of calls over the following hours and days. We may have appeared like an emerging, professional social business, but our 1300 number was just a regular phone line diverted to one of our team's mobile phones. The result of this, and the fact that this particular team member was juggling uni and a part-time job on the side of Thankyou, was hundreds of missed calls. Epic fail!

Day two's segment was just as generous and in total, we received 13-and-a-half minutes of airtime over the two days. The camera crew and another producer later told us they had never seen that happen before. This coverage was the start of what would become an incredible relationship with *Sunrise*, who would go on to update their viewers on our story more than 16 times in the years that followed; we hope they'll continue to support us for many years to come. You'll find that first clip (and the rest of our *Sunrise* stories) on our YouTube channel.

After the *Sunrise* piece aired, more cafés and independent stores began ordering our water and as a result, we grew by hundreds of stockists. A group called Provender, who own hundreds of vending machines, came on board.

We even received an order from a lady for 44 pallets of water – our biggest single order to date!

We were a little shattered when we called to confirm, only to discover that she thought a pallet was the same as a box. Forty-four boxes is a little different to 44 pallets – by about 75,864 bottles – but we were thrilled by the growing support for our cause nonetheless.

Best of all, the cherry on the cake was that the hosts of *Sunrise*, David "Kochie" Koch and Melissa Doyle, had a surprise for us. They announced it live on national TV and we were blown away when we heard the news: *"Jetstar Airways have just announced that they will be stocking Thankyou Water on all flights!"* This was beyond incredible news, because it meant that not only would it bring about a huge increase in distribution, but also that our water was about to officially go international.

Unfortunately, this deal didn't end up coming to fruition – and sadly, it wasn't the only disappointment to come after our shining moment. After this huge media storm, we went back to the retailers we had unsuccessfully pitched to previously and tried again.

"Remember how you said we needed more awareness? Well, check this out!" we said proudly. This was followed up with a question to which we were quietly confident of a positive response: "Will you consider stocking us now?" Their response was swift and brutal. Using slightly different words, they said we were a "one-hit wonder". We were up against multinational brands investing millions of dollars into continual marketing campaigns. So, in their view, almost 14 minutes of prime-time television coverage wasn't enough for them to justify ranging our product.

THE GAME-CHANGING CAMPAIGN

After three years of knockbacks, setbacks and discouraging stories that left us with only a couple of water wells funded, a team of almost burnt-out volunteers, a 'glimmer of light' deal with Australia Post and a one-hit wonder segment on national television, we were disheartened, to say the least.

However, it was obvious that we had to do something different to get a result that we hadn't yet achieved. I figure you'll probably forget that sentence so I've come up with something a little more memorable, hence the chapter title: sometimes, you have to high-five the status quo in the face – with a chair. So we did.

We booked a meeting with 7-Eleven Australia for July 4, 2011. We picked them of all retailers, because they were engaging with people in our target market like no other and from our perspective, they had some room in the fridge.

Leading up to that date was months of preparation on our end, which culminated in the launch of a social media campaign exactly two weeks before our meeting. On a mid-June morning at around 10am, we posted a bold message and video on our Facebook page as a 'call to action' to our supporters: "Two weeks from today we are presenting to 7-Eleven, but we don't want to walk in there and just tell them how great our product is. We want them to know that people are going to actually buy it."

We then asked people to upload a video or post directly to 7-Eleven Australia's Facebook wall. Our hope was that if we could motivate people to pledge their support for the product, 7-Eleven might take us seriously. So what happened next? We posted the message and then anxiously refreshed 7-Eleven's Facebook page every couple of minutes. There was a nervous few moments initially when it didn't look like anything was happening. But what followed that day was an absolute influx of messages from our supporters. Hundreds of posts went up, hour after hour. By 4pm that day, there were at least 400 posts on their Facebook wall, with more appearing each minute.

A few nights later, we were featured on Channel Ten's *The Project*, one of the most popular nightly news panel shows in Australia. They planned to cover our story broadly, but said they couldn't mention the campaign, as it was a little controversial. *The Project* ended up running a five-and-a-half-minute feature on Thankyou Water; shortly after the broadcast, we were trending on Twitter! At the end of the segment two of the hosts, Charlie Pickering and Carrie Bickmore, were talking about us when Carrie finished off with, "Hey everyone, head to Facebook as there is a big petition going on." Carrie, if you are reading this book: thank you for saying that! What followed was unbelievable; 7-Eleven's Facebook page was flooded with even more support for Thankyou Water.

The next morning, the phone rang: it was the buyer we had been dealing with at 7-Eleven. I was a little nervous about his reaction to our campaign, so I let his call go to voicemail. I found the courage to call back and he said, "Congratulations, you've got the entire company glued to Facebook."

I should note that we had a countdown timer on our website until the meeting and a section that asked, "Would you like to see Thankyou Water in 7-Eleven?" Those who clicked the 'yes' button were transported to the 7-Eleven Australia Facebook page, where people could pledge their support. There was also a 'no' button. The buyer had noticed this on the website and commented to me, "It's a bit cheeky that the 'no' button doesn't go anywhere." I told him that it wasn't a strategic ploy; we just didn't know where to send people if they clicked 'no'! He said he looked forward to our meeting and we ended our first phone call on good terms. My gut feeling was that he wasn't as excited about this campaign as we were, because we had just created a potential headache for him and the rest of the 7-Eleven Australia team.

In the lead-up to our meeting, the campaign grew in awareness with more media covering the story and more people uploading messages and videos of themselves singing, dancing and even rapping to show their support for our product. There's a compilation video on our YouTube channel that shows what I'm talking about; it was insane!

WHEN YOU'VE DONE SOMETHING REALLY RIGHT... OR REALLY WRONG

A few days later, I got another call from the buyer to ask if we could come in early for the meeting. He also asked that we didn't announce the new meeting time on Facebook, because there were rumours that people were planning to turn up on the front lawn on meeting day to show their support for Thankyou Water. We didn't plan that!

It turns out that in addition to the media and social media attention, 7-Eleven Australia's main hotline number was also getting hit with a steady stream of customer calls requesting the product.

We agreed to an earlier appointment, as we felt we were as prepared as we ever could be. We walked into that meeting, not knowing what to expect. When we sat down, the buyer offered an apology that the CEO couldn't make it. You know you've done something right (or really wrong) when that happens.

Over the next hour, we presented a sound commercial case. After three years of similar meetings, we'd learned many lessons that had helped fine-tune our pitch. We also knew that, naturally, there were many commercial questions these guys needed answered. It could have gone either way – they could have easily disliked us immensely after the cheeky tactic we used to get their attention, or they could have recognised our passion for what it was. Thankfully, they seemed to be just as excited as we were, because they too could see the potential of the product in their stores. As a result, something remarkable happened that day.

After our one-hour presentation, they sat there looking genuinely impressed. We'd presented a proper commercial offer, just like any other supplier would have, but we also put forward an opportunity for them to make a global impact by doing something that was core to their business – selling drinks.

Justine, Jarryd and I left that meeting on a high, thinking that maybe, just maybe, we'd finally reached a retailer that could see our vision and wanted to support it. Three days later, on 7/7/11 (an uncanny date) at 3:34pm, I received a one-line email from my contact at 7-Eleven Australia. It simply said: "Please call."

The reason I mention the time is because at 3pm that day, I had begun my shift at Vodafone, which was my second job at the time. I took a toilet break and I called my contact back in one of the shopping centre service hallways. It was a quick phone call but one of the most memorable moments of my life. Their answer was positive – they wanted to range Thankyou Water. They'd considered not just our campaign, but also the commercial aspect and the entire package, and they were as excited as we were. Needless to say, I found it a little hard returning to my shift to sell phones and deal with difficult customers until 9pm that night!

Within a week, the three of us were in their office for the final sign-off meeting. The way their team backed our idea actually caught us off guard. They didn't want any strings attached or any special conditions in the agreement; they just wanted to help us get the concept 'out there'. We loved the fact that their team really believed in our vision.

Finally, it seemed that three years of persistence had paid off. Our team worked out that we'd sent and received over 25,000 emails to potential retailers and stockists in the years leading up to this moment. Each email represented the tireless hours that each of us had invested to help see our idea become a reality. We never could have imagined that it would have taken this long or been this hard.

We finished up our final meeting with 7-Eleven Australia, which was held on a Wednesday, with the aim of launching in stores the following Monday. But as we left, we had no idea what would be waiting for us at our office.

AN UNEXPECTED LETTER DELIVERS YET ANOTHER BLOW

When I arrived back at my desk, still on a high after signing our first major retailing agreement, there was a letter waiting for me. It looked a little bit official and I thought that maybe it was a parking fine. I opened the letter and it was from Consumer Affairs Victoria. To my horror, the letter was not good. In fact, it was downright terrifying. It stated we had been trading without a fundraising licence. As a result, it said we must cease trading immediately or face further action.

It was true that we had never obtained a fundraising licence. But this was because we had never asked for the public to donate to us – instead, we sold a product and then funded charitable projects with our profit. We didn't 'fundraise' and therefore didn't ever see the need to have this licence.

I called our lawyers as I knew there must have been some mistake. They reviewed the contents of the letter and our lawyer said we would need to pause our upcoming launch with 7-Eleven Australia – the one that was meant to take place the following Monday – as it was going to take up to 10 weeks to sort out the predicament we were in.

He then delivered the worse news: not only would we have to postpone the launch, but we couldn't sell any more product through any stockist we had. We were beyond devastated. We decided to wait until the next morning to make the call to 7-Eleven. It was a pretty quiet night at home that evening. Usually I'm the positive one, but this night, I just felt defeated – I couldn't believe that on the brink of success, once again, we were dealt a massive blow.

However, Justine was the opposite. She was so sure we'd get through this and said positively, "This time tomorrow night, everything will be sorted and we'll be able go ahead with the launch. Just watch." Now, there is a saying that your wife is always right, but I felt that in this instance, she was just being overly optimistic. This was a big issue and one that I didn't think would be sorted out overnight.

The next morning before work, I put a call through to a business mentor. I explained the situation and he cracked it. Not at me, but at Consumer Affairs – and at the fact that our legal advice had been to pull the launch. He felt that not only was the timing uncanny (a competitor probably raised the complaint with Consumer Affairs), but he was convinced that we absolutely weren't fundraising due to our social enterprise business model. He called the lawyers and by 9.30am we had a pretty serious letter sent off to Consumer Affairs. It was on.

By 4pm that afternoon, we had worked through the mess and while we were in fact justified in not having the licence, we had ascertained that the path of least resistance was to apply for one in any event (we'll change that stuff when we have some more time). We put the application through and were advised that we could move forward with the launch and continue trading, as the licence would be approved in the coming weeks. Let's just say Justine was smiling that night.

A few days later, both *Sunrise* and *The Project* covered the launch with 7-Eleven and over the next week, we had write-ups and interviews across numerous media publications. The media and the public were celebrating the decision and it wasn't long before our product outsold Evian in their fridges, then both Evian and Cool Ridge (another major brand on the market) combined! It was unbelievable to see the rapid growth in our business. We were still pinching ourselves that it was actually real.

Two months later, we were invited to attend 7-Eleven Australia's national conference at which the board, head office employees and franchisees were all present. It was one of our first-ever corporate conferences and it set the bar pretty high. Picture a giant Slurpee machine offering unlimited refills with a dozen new flavours that haven't yet hit the market – including the classic New Zealand (quickly adopted by Aussies) dessert, Pavlova.

I was asked to speak to the 1000-plus people in the main auditorium about the Thankyou Water concept. If that wasn't nerve-wracking enough, I had a glance at the run sheet for the day and saw that the speaker lineup included world famous cricketer Glenn McGrath, leading international comedian Ahn Do… and me.

When the CEO of 7-Eleven Australia invited me on stage, I knew I couldn't let nerves get in the way of this moment. What 7-Eleven had done by ranging our product was remarkable and I couldn't thank them enough. But at the end of the talk, I shared with the franchisees that I had a number on my mind; a target that I challenged them to play a part in reaching.

I said that if together, we could hit the rate of selling 10 units per store per day, then each franchisee would go on to help 24 people get access to safe water. While that figure sounds small, as a combined family of franchisees, that would mean 7-Eleven Australia would help over 15,000 people every year. The room erupted in applause. They weren't applauding me, but they had just realised they were about to be part of something so much bigger than themselves.

Where did we get the 10 units per store per day number from? Well, I'd read somewhere that the market leader Mount Franklin (owned by Coca-Cola Amatil) was selling around that volume every day. Right after I shared the ambitious target from the stage, I could see one of their executive team lean over to another and say, "They're not even selling one." That was spot on – we were selling around 0.6 bottles per day on average across all 7-Eleven stores. To boost that figure to 10 was an extremely ambitious target but regardless, 7-Eleven backed our boldness and made a decision to set our figure as the benchmark for the business to work towards. Over the coming months, our sales continued to grow. We took one of 7-Eleven's board members to see the projects in the field, and we then created a video to show the franchisees the impact they were making through stocking and selling our product.

From there, 7-Eleven Australia decided they wanted to create a bigger impact and made a strategic decision to drop their own home-brand water, Munch, so they could dedicate that space in their fridges to more Thankyou Water. This bold move meant we had the lowest price point water in their stores, without affecting our margins, and we had as much fridge space as our main competitor.

The whole industry still probably scratches its head as to why 7-Eleven Australia made that decision, but we were thrilled. 7-Eleven were committed to making the biggest impact possible. We were already outselling other brands, and we went on to hit that target of 10 units per store per day.

Together, over the following two years (as at financial year 2014), we have raised over $1 million to fund access to safe water for over 100,000 people. The incredible impact of this partnership continues to grow every day.

THE VALUE OF ONE IDEA

The 7-Eleven campaign was a game changer for us, and we believe for them. While the campaign could have easily looked like we were trying to back 7-Eleven Australia into a corner and force their hand, I can assure you we weren't. We were tired of trying to convince retailers that 'if' they stocked our product the public would support it, the media would get behind it and it would sell like crazy. The campaign was our attempt to prove those things first, so 7-Eleven wouldn't have to take our word for it.

One morning, I was in the waiting room of Retail Zoo, the parent company of Boost Juice. There was a big, bold quote on the wall that proclaimed, "An idea isn't worth much; its value is found in its execution." It's a profound statement and it really sums up the first three years of our journey.

We believed our idea was great and attempted to sell it over and over again with unsuccessful results, but it wasn't until we changed the way we presented the idea that we finally caught a break. That campaign gained Thankyou some media attention, particularly in the marketing space. It was the first campaign of its kind and that was part of its design. To disrupt the status quo you have to attempt things that haven't been done before. It's obvious, but sometimes so obvious that you miss it. If you are attempting to execute your idea the exact way someone else did, then you are not going to change anything; you're simply playing by the rules that have already been set.

So don't get caught up just on the idea itself – no matter how brilliant it may be – but focus on its execution. And when executing your idea, remember that just because it's never been done before doesn't mean it can't be done. We certainly never let little concerns like 'experience' and 'proven results' get in our way!

It turns out, this would not be the last time we'd high-five the status quo in the face – with a chair. Better still, our next attempt would go on to grab global attention.

SOME THOUGHTS TO TAKE AWAY:

ONE. People often don't see what you see in your idea. It's your job to prove it. Business plans, words and impressive presentations do not compare to a real life proof of concept, which is all about getting them to actually see what you can see.

TWO. Your idea itself doesn't hold much value; it's your ability to find a unique way to execute your idea that is your 'secret sauce'.

THREE. Sometimes – in fact, often times – you have to be prepared to go against the way things have always been done. Be brave – your lack of experience in challenging the status quo may be the greatest strength you have.

FOUR. When you are challenging the way things have always been done, it might take lawyers a little longer to get comfortable.

CHAPTER 1.6

Build A Great Team To Achieve A Great Dream

Teamwork makes the dream work.

This is the title of a great book by John C Maxwell. It so brilliantly sums up what I want to say about our team at Thankyou that I had to borrow it.

Changing stuff and making your idea a reality isn't a one-person show. Success is sometimes mistakenly attributed to just one person, but in reality it takes an extraordinary, committed and passionate team to build any great dream.

We don't always get that impression when we read 'the book' or hear 'the speaker' share ideas that have been successful. These books are often written by a single person (like this one, for example), which means we automatically attribute the idea's success to that one person, and not the entire team who worked hard behind the scenes to make things happen.

When we think about a company like Virgin, many of us consider Richard Branson as the genius behind the brand. While he's got an impressive set of talents, so do his 50,000-strong workforce, spread across 300 businesses that are each managed by gifted individual leaders. Together, they make Virgin and together they create something great.

Making sure you build the right team is fundamental for ensuring you have what it takes to make your idea a reality. Often we attribute the idea of 'team' to a group of people we are directly working with in our day-to-day life. But this is a limited view, and may cause you to fall into the trap of failing to develop a great team until you're ready to start your organisation.

It doesn't matter what your dream looks like – its success will require you to build a great team, the sooner the better.

For me, the assumption that your team is a wider group than just your direct staff was an obvious concept, so I was caught off guard at our staff Christmas party a few years back. I had just gone around the room and individually thanked every person while sharing stories about each of our team, and then I thanked the wider team (spouses and partners) for their support.

Afterwards, several of our staff's partners came up and commended me for thanking them. Many of them said they had never felt so valued for being a 'partner', and very few said they had even considered themselves part of our team. Perhaps because Jarryd, Justine and I all work with our spouses (Jarryd's wife Jess now works with Thankyou), we realise the impact having complete support from your spouse or your partner has. It's incredible!

I've learned how true John C Maxwell's statement is, that teamwork does make the dream work, so it's up to you to build your team – and it goes much wider than you may think. The first group to consider is your personal support team. I am who I am because of the love, support and encouragement of those around me. We hero the self-made person but rarely are they actually self-made; we are not designed to do life alone and while some of us may have a big supporter base and some of us may only have one person backing us – we all need someone.

FAMILY AND FRIENDS: YOUR INNER CIRCLE

My most important 'diary' appointments are not the 'big' meetings I have; they are always exciting, but they come and they go. It's the time I get to spend with people I value highest – my family, friends and mentors – that matters most. Don't make the mistake of thinking you don't have time for them. I've definitely made the mistake of leaving these people till last many times before, and it takes constant awareness to stop from slipping into those habits again.

Now, for many people reading this, you may recognise that your inner circle can often be the source of your greatest criticisms and discouragements. I've been lucky to have a family who sometimes thought my ideas were a little "out there", but have always made the decision to believe in me regardless.

This may not be your experience but here's something to think about: you are someone's family, you are someone's friend and you are part of someone's team. In what ways do you show your family, friends or team members that you believe in them? Belief is a powerful thing. People achieve great things when they know that others believe they can.

I have learned over time that true friends are those who support you and believe in you even if – *especially* if – they think some of your ideas and behaviours are crazy. True friends are also extremely hard to find. They are the ones who stand with you for those mountain-top experiences, but they are also there when you walk through the darkest valleys. They are the people who, when you walk away after catching up with them, you don't feel drained, but you feel refreshed.

The busier you get in life, the harder it is to keep friends like this. You have to be intentional.

Often we think that family and friends will understand when we're constantly tied up at work or consumed with implementing a new business idea, but relationships go both ways. Don't forget to invest into what is most important.

I know I wouldn't be where I am today without Justine. Her role in my life outside of work is my wife; she's my biggest support. She's held me up when I've felt down, she's encouraged me to push through when all I have wanted to do is give up. While I admit this does sound like I'm trying to win massive brownie points, the real intention of these words is to be open with you and say that it's simply not possible for anyone to do it alone. Regardless of whether or not you have a partner or spouse, you're not meant to walk the journey on your own – the support of key family members and friends is crucial.

THE ONLY PROVEN FORM OF TIME TRAVEL

Here's something you probably didn't know: mentoring is the only proven form of time travel you can readily access. During a catch-up over coffee with your mentor, you can learn one piece of wisdom that may have taken that person 20 years to discover. This doesn't apply only to people in business; it is a universal concept that is relevant to virtually everyone.

When I look back over my journey, I can see that mentoring was a fundamental component that helped get me to where I am today. Mentors come in many different shapes and sizes. They may provide some technical advice, but generally they are more interested in your development.

This is what I love about great mentors: they don't do it to be recognised. They do it because they genuinely believe in you and want to see you go further than they've ever gone. They are selflessly willing to gift you pearls of wisdom and advice that may have taken them a lifetime of experience to build. Their secret weapon is that they can help shift your perspective, without you even realising a change in perspective was needed.

I've been blessed over my life to have numerous mentors who have played small to significant roles in my life. It almost feels like I'm dishonouring all of these people if I only share stories of one or two, when I know there have been over a dozen mentors who have invested in me over the years (and still do today). I could easily fill another book if I shared my best moments with each of them!

My dad, who's been one of my greatest mentors, once had the boldness to walk up to the guest speaker at a business breakfast he was attending. He explained that his son (me!) had to complete a year 10 work experience assignment for school and he was wondering if this particular executive would consider taking me on at his organisation.

That speaker wasn't just your average breakfast speaker. His name was George, and he was the CEO of one of Australia's largest billion-dollar businesses. I have no doubt that George was caught off guard by the request. He explained that he'd never had a work experience student before (which is understandable for a CEO) but that he would consider it and get back to him. To my dad's excitement, George later said he would accept me as his first work experience student.

I'll never forget my first day. I was a 15-year-old kid with a high-pitched voice spending the week in a CEO's office, and I couldn't quite believe what I was experiencing. I remember sitting quietly in the first meeting and within minutes, the people around the table were talking about hundreds of millions of dollars without even blinking.

As they dropped "400 million this" and "300 million that", I could feel a shift brewing. What proceeded was a week full of moments that continued to change my perspective.

Ever since that week, George has kept walking this journey with me and has been an incredible mentoring figure in my life. Throughout many points in our journey, he has helped shift my perspective. Just recently George asked me to come and speak to his executive team, which was a huge honour when you consider the fact that I was once the work experience kid.

Just before I got up to speak, I updated him on the latest happenings at Thankyou. I mentioned that over the past few weeks, I'd given five to eight talks per week at different events, mainly corporate gatherings. I thought at the time that it was quite a lot of speaking to commit to, while simultaneously running Thankyou. Mentally and physically, I was maxed out: how could I do any more than I was doing?

Then George casually dropped that he'd just got back from doing 160 talks over four weeks at events in multiple countries – 160 talks! In this moment, my perspective changed. Now, I know George doesn't do that every month, but it wasn't completely out of the ordinary either; it was one of two month-long talking tours he was doing in the back half of the year. It's moments like this that I realise my half-dozen talks per week may not be my limit.

GETTING COMFORTABLE WITH DISCOMFORT

The least comfortable part of the mentoring process, but probably the most important part, is when your mentor calls your blind spots to challenge and refine you. It's called a blind spot because it's more than likely invisible to you and it can be really uncomfortable when it's brought to your attention. Throughout the years I've seen the value of this and have learned to embrace it, but in the early days I really struggled with this particular aspect of the mentoring process.

In the beginning, after we landed our first few big deals and received a couple of strong media hits, I remember being so excited to tell one of my closest mentors, Neil, about our progress. We caught up for breakfast and I shared with him about the good things that were happening.

While I was talking he seemed interested, but it was a different level of excitement than what I'd encountered when I told other people. When I finished, he acknowledged the success we'd had but quickly moved on with a few questions. Then he said, "As I'm hearing you talk and as I've watched you along the journey, I can see some weaknesses in your leadership. If we don't work through this, you'll cap the potential of Thankyou." I remember thinking, "What! Did you not just hear about all the awesome stuff I was talking about?" Let's just say I wasn't in a hurry to catch up again. However, over the coming months, everything that Neil mentioned played out in front of me. A large part of me only wanted to admit that he was 50 per cent right, but he wasn't. He was pretty much 100 per cent correct.

Neil called my blind spots. He challenged me because he believed in me and wanted to see me refine my skills in order to move further forwards. I once confessed to Neil that I really didn't like catching up with him at the start, as it was too confronting, but I grew to realise that I needed it and it made me stronger.

After Neil had been mentoring me for a while, he invited me to go with him on what would be my first-ever international trip. He was speaking in New Zealand and I was travelling with him. On the way to the breakfast event, Neil informed me that he was going to get me to say a few words.

I remember the nerves hitting me, but as he threw me the microphone I had no choice but to rise to the challenge. I later found out that he'd planned this the whole way along.

This story proves my next point: a great mentor will look for opportunities to help challenge and refine you. This would be the first of many moments that Neil would present to 'refine' my leadership skills. It's taught me to be ready at any moment and to be confident in my ability to say something that sounds half-decent without any preparation.

It's important to realise that mentors are not there to fix your problems or make your decisions; they are there to encourage and give you their opinion based on their experience. It's up to you to find out the answer on your own. That's why the best mentors often have the frustrating but ultimately rewarding habit of answering your question with a question.

What does a mentor get in return, for investing so much time and effort into you and your ideas? Sometimes, you can pay for mentoring. But I've found many of my mentors are not looking for a monetary return – they are looking for something much more important than that.

There is a satisfaction that arises when you know that your life's work, your journey, your lessons learned could go on to help propel someone else's journey. There is satisfaction in seeing a younger person or someone that is less experienced reach their full potential and at the same time, know that you've been able to play a small part in that journey. Thankyou is where it is today because of the dozens of mentors who have believed in me, challenged me, refined me, encouraged me and helped change my perspective.

I have heard it said that the greatest way to repay a mentor is to return the favour to others. Every mentor wants to know that they are leaving a legacy and that this legacy doesn't stop with you. They are investing in you so that you can invest in others. They are investing in you because others invested in them. It's kind of an unwritten code.

FINDING YOUR IDEAL MENTORING MATCH

You may already have some great mentors in your life, or you may still be searching for your ideal mentoring match. If the latter is more familiar for you, my advice is to write a letter to someone who you think could be a good fit with what you're trying to do.

I suggest that you write a letter because it shows you're willing to take some time to reach out, rather than just typing an email or sending a tweet. They need to know you value their time. In the letter, introduce yourself and ask if they'd be willing for you to buy them a quick coffee or lunch. Do not ask them if they would be your mentor! Even after the first catch-up, I wouldn't drop the 'mentor' word.

There are two reasons for this. The first is, it sounds like too much commitment and most of the people you are chasing to mentor you are already time-poor. The second reason is that you don't know yet if you actually want them to mentor or advise you. The start of a mentor/advisor relationship is almost like a first date. You're trying to get to know them as much as they are trying to get to know you. It's important to let things build organically. If your first catch-up was worth it, ask for a second a few weeks or months later. If they are up for it, you're off to a good start.

Now that I reflect, I don't think I've ever asked anyone if they would officially mentor me;

it's always been a natural progression. Over the years, I've had mentors who have moved overseas, moved careers and had other changes in their lives, which have naturally ended our mentoring. A mentoring setup isn't a signed contract; it's just having a coach through certain parts of life. As the years go by, some coaches are there for the journey; others are just for a season. No one wants to be locked in either way.

My final thought for you on mentors is an aspect of the arrangement that I'm still working on. We have to be careful not to let our own pride, insecurities and feelings stop us from walking a healthy mentoring journey. It's not always easy to book in that next catch-up, but it's so important. Your idea, your story and your journey will be helped or hindered based on your ability to stay humble and let others challenge and refine you.

There's an old proverb that talks about wisdom being found in a multitude of counsellors. The key word to note here is 'multitude'. There have been times where I've had two mentors give me literally opposite opinions on the same idea or topic. At first, this scenario really stressed me out. How could two people so smart and developed be saying polar-opposite things?

The reality is, they are speaking from their own experience. We live in a world where everyone's judgments are based on their own experiences – and no two people have ever had the exact same experience. Remember that this journey is about you discovering what you need to do, not implementing 100 per cent of what someone tells you. By having multiple mentors, it helps you refine your plans and decisions. Good mentors expect you to make your own decisions, based on your own conviction. If you are simply cutting and pasting 100 per cent of what another person is saying, no matter how wise or experienced they are, you won't end up where you need to be.

Instead, you need to take the best of what you've heard. Sometimes when you have contradictory suggestions, it's the best thing for you – because you will be forced to make your final decision on your own, with conviction and good reasoning.

BUILDING YOUR IDEAL WORKING TEAM

Changing stuff and making your ideas a reality isn't something you can afford to do alone. Even with great friends, family and mentors you still need to tackle each day with others around you. Teams exist because everyone individually has strengths and weakness but together you can be strong. It's the sum of the parts more than individuals alone that have the power and capacity to truly effect change. I'm the lucky guy who gets to lead our team and write the book about our journey, but in reality, I'm only one small piece of the puzzle. Over the years, it has taken a team of incredibly dedicated, committed and passionate people to build Thankyou.

Between the three of us who co-founded Thankyou (Justine, Jarryd and myself), each of us with our own unique talents and strengths, we have discovered a perfect dynamic to lead and guide the vision of our organisation. We cover each other's weaknesses and champion each other's strengths. Looking at the diverse skill set between the three of us, we actually couldn't be less alike, but I think that's why we work together so well. The unity we have as a leadership team comes from both balanced discussion and healthy disagreement.

Our organisation's focus on teamwork has been driven by Justine's passion. In the early days, I never fully understood just how many people it would take to pull off our vision but she was adamant from the start that we needed to find as many great people as possible.

Early on, Justine convinced Jarryd and I of the need for volunteers. I say convinced because we thought, somewhat confidently, that we could just do it all ourselves. From out of nowhere, Justine found a group of volunteers and then got them involved in helping drive the vision. Some of these initial volunteers include Pete, Kirk, Wesley, Tim, April and Jan-Lee, who went on to become key staff members in our organisation.

Jarryd and I still have a lot of input when it comes to hiring people, but we've respected and supported Justine's decisions in this area over the years because she has a natural intuition when it comes to people. People who come in always comment on our culture, which has been established as a result of making sure we get the right people 'on the bus'. We know that it can only take one person to disrupt a great culture. While Justine has had a big focus on our people and systems, she has also got an amazing creative flair. People often comment that they're blown away with our videos, design, products and our multiple world-first marketing campaigns, all led by Justine.

I remember once telling her I had this cool idea that we could just make soap bars to fund health and hygiene training. She smiled and put some other ideas down on paper. If you see our incredible body care product range today, you'll see why we're glad it wasn't just my 'creativity' involved in our product development.

I am so grateful for the vision and creativity that Justine brings to Thankyou, and I'm just as grateful for the strengths Jarryd brings to the table – the decisions he's made and his incredible eye for detail have helped build Thankyou into what it is today. Jarryd and I go all the way back to a networking event in 1995. We were both around the age of five years old – that networking event was in fact our prep (first year of formal schooling in Australia) orientation day.

Jarryd's role has become insanely complicated and detailed over the years. My grandfather, who passed away in 2013, was a very successful businessman and his most important piece of advice for me was, "Find someone you trust to look after the finances. It will make or break your business." Jarryd is that guy and Justine and I both trust him implicitly.

We'll never forget one Saturday morning, back in the beginning of our journey, when we fronted up for a flight only to discover that one of our team had made an error with the booking. At the counter, they told us it was going to cost $600 to get on the flight. We were about to run a huge event that day (which ended up making us over $15,000 in sales) and we quite simply had no other choice but to be there. We had to pay cash (typical budget airline) and so I went to the ATM machine to withdraw money. The withdraw limit was $200 so I had to make three withdrawals.

Begrudgingly, we paid for the flight and it wasn't long before I got a text from Jarryd, who wanted to know why I withdrew cash from an ATM that wasn't our bank "because it cost us $6 in fees". Keep in mind this is 9am on a Saturday morning! He figured the $600 had been withdrawn for the event cash float. You can imagine his feelings when I had to break the news to him that we actually had to spend that $600 on emergency flights...

Jarryd has an undying commitment to making sure every cent is well spent, not wasted. He has brought so much sound advice and strategy to the vision. We look up to him for his wisdom and ability to carry so much responsibility at such a young age. Jarryd is in charge of multimillion-dollar budgets and operations and now manages people who are many years his senior.

I think the three of us have all felt that if you put any one of us in the other's role, we'd probably quit, because we are not cut out for it. That's a good sign. Building your direct team is all about making sure people are playing to their strengths.

As we've grown, it's been about adding more and more working team members to strengthen us. You can only do what you can do. If the three of us were the only team members now, we wouldn't have anything worth writing about. Our incredible executive team, now working alongside the three of us, has brought increased strength to the management of the organisation. We've had board members join who are bringing years and years of experience. I feel like each week, we've got someone new joining us and it just keeps getting better.

Pulling a team together is one thing, but working as a team is the next challenge. Modern society is pretty good at setting the agenda for workplace hierarchies. We naturally position a CEO or MD right up at the top of the chain and then proceed to rank all other roles according to importance in a neat reporting line below that. If you're from the corporate world, you might be all too used to the under-handed politics and power plays that take place as people attempt to move up the ladder.

At Thankyou, there's something we fundamentally believe about teamwork that has been part of our success. We have an organisational structure like every business and on paper, I'm sitting at the top of that. But really, that's just words written on a piece of paper. We honour every person for the unique gifts that they have and bring to our team. As an example, let me tell you about our creative designers, Wesley and Jan-Lee. Wesley volunteered above and beyond at the beginning of our journey, and Jan-Lee was fresh out of university when she joined us but both of them produce work that ranks up there with the best in the industry. From my experience, these two are world-class creative geniuses and what they bring to Thankyou is something that I could never, ever attempt to bring.

I'd love to finish this example by talking about what I'm good at that my team are not, but they are all pretty amazing and I'm still trying to figure out what I actually do at Thankyou (my title says Managing Director, so I attempt to manage the direction as best I can). What is great about a healthy team is that if we each bring our unique abilities to the table, together we will see the dream become a reality. When you truly honour the gifts and talents that each team member has – instead of their organisational rank – then you develop unity in your team that will position you to achieve incredible things.

I am a big believer of dreams within dreams and dreamers within dreamers. It's my dream to lead our team, but others dream about creating the best design, developing ground-breaking marketing campaigns, implementing efficient systems and processes, setting in place innovative development practices in the field, and the list goes on. When we combine our dreams, something amazing happens and together we see the overall vision become a reality.

As you grow, as an individual or as an organisation, there will be areas in which you lack expertise and resources. This is when it becomes important to involve 'advisors' as part of your working team. They may not be part of your day-to-day activities, but they surround you with advice on areas of their expertise. Lawyers, accountants, marketers, strategists, business consultants and many other types of advisors will add significant value to your journey and form an invaluable part of your working team.

STRATEGIC PARTNERSHIPS TAKE YOUR VISION FURTHER

If you look at some of the most successful businesses in the world, their success isn't a result of them doing everything on their own. Rather, their success comes about from building great partnerships.

If you want to implement your idea, in whatever shape or form, I firmly believe the key to its success can be found in partnership.

Thankyou partners with some of Australia's leading food, water and body care manufacturers to produce market-leading products. We don't own our own factories and we don't ever want to – we contract manufacturers. Why? Because our manufacturers have been making products like ours since before most of our team members were even born. They've already made the mistakes and through that, figured out what works and what doesn't, which means we don't have to go through that process, yet we get to benefit from the expertise they've developed. With their support, we can scale up to become a large brand overnight, with the ability to meet the demand we're creating by partnering with the biggest retailers in the country.

When it comes to legal, accounting, advisory and other business services, we partner with the best because we want the best results. Every level of our business is built on great partnerships. When it comes to the field and the projects we fund, it's no different. From day one we wanted to work with the best of the best because we want the most sustainable results on the ground.

There is a widespread negative public perception when it comes to prominent charities, with many believing that due to expensive overheads, a significant portion of donated funds won't actually reach the need. In Australia, we are lucky because most of the prominent NGOs (non-government organisations) have an incredibly low ratio percentage of administration costs, in relation to development expenditure.

We work using a project-by-project model and in the past we have worked with recognised organisations including the Red Cross, World Vision, Oxfam, The Salvation Army, UNHCR, UNICEF, Care Australia and Samaritan's Purse. We will accept proposals from any NGO that specialises in development and meets our strict list of detailed criteria. Provided the organisation fulfils our requirements, reports correctly and our visit proves that the reports and the tangible solutions add up, we'll consider funding more of their projects going forwards.

I'm often asked, "Why don't you do the work in the field yourselves?" Our answer: we are about changing the game, but we aren't about reinventing the wheel. Nicolette (who I mentioned earlier as part of our founding team) was so passionate about strong, sustainable development that she funnelled all of our "we want to change the world" enthusiasm into a sophisticated partnership model that was sustainable and would allow us to make a lasting impact.

From the start, we knew that partnering with established NGOs would result in us being able to make sure communities were given the best chance of experiencing long-term, sustainable change through the programs we fund. There are a couple of reasons for this, the first one being that our project partners are local and live within the area for anywhere between 5 and 15 years.

Furthermore, they're experienced in development. This means that every project we fund is tailored to each different community, to make sure needs are met effectively. At the heart of this approach is the idea of *empowerment*, which I touched on at the beginning of this book. Working with experts in development means we're confident that each community we serve alongside our project partners is empowered to play crucial roles within their own development.

The importance of making sure your team includes strong partners was driven home during our first project trip to Cambodia. We were heading to see a well that we had funded in one of the provinces. As we walked into the village, I couldn't help but notice that there were in fact already a few existing wells in and around this particular community. At that point, I felt like I'd 'sprung' our project partner.

Before I got too upset, I tapped the project manager on the shoulder and said, "Why are we funding wells in this community when we can see three existing wells here already?" He pointed to the first well and said, "See that one? When it was installed by a charity, it was dug in during wet season, which means that in dry season when the community really needs water, there is none." He pointed to the second well and explained how that particular well had hit a bed of arsenic, so if the community drank from it they would get arsenic poisoning. Enough said. We were in shock as he explained the third well had a mechanical fault, and that the cost of fixing it would be more than the cost of sinking a whole new sustainable well.

The crazy thing about this is that there are three groups around the world claiming to have 'helped' these people, yet this community still didn't have access to safe water.

The well we had funded was quite expensive, but built into that cost was initial surveys, to determine water table level and ensure there was no presence of arsenic. It was a proper, sustainable solution with locally sourced parts. It also included a provision for ongoing staffing costs, since our project partner had made a commitment to stay in the area for five to seven years, until they knew that the community was fully self-sustainable from a water, sanitation and education perspective.

We also met the village water committee, who had been trained on repairs in the event that the well might break down. This community now had a fighting chance of long-term access to safe water.

Still today, I get upset thinking about the other three unusable wells and the amount of wasted resources involved. The sad truth is that these situations are a reality when well-intended development projects are poorly executed. There are so many well-meaning people wanting to help those in need, offering quick fixes that are cheap but are not sustainable or properly planned out.

What's our secret to our success so far? It's simple: teamwork. Build a great team, both internally and externally through strong strategic partnerships – and you'll be well on your way to building a great dream.

SOME THOUGHTS TO TAKE AWAY:

ONE. Never in our lives can we afford to get to a point where we think we know it all. Be humble, be teachable and always keep learning.

TWO. It's not possible to make your ideas and dreams a reality by doing it alone – but build a great team and you'll achieve a great dream.

THREE. Find outstanding mentors. Mentorship is literally a form of time travel. The greatest mentors won't get too excited about what you do (like everyone else around you), but they'll call it how they see it and challenge you to be better.

FOUR. Don't try to reinvent the wheel; leverage off partnerships with like-minded organisations or groups to achieve great outcomes.

FIVE. Complaining about your workload to the CEO of one of the country's biggest companies will probably give you some perspective.

CHAPTER 1.7
Facing The Giants

Here's something you might find interesting:
Thankyou Water was never meant to be Thankyou Water.

From the word go, we dreamed of things that will be written many chapters on from the last chapter in this book. But the greatest brands and movements all started somewhere and for us, we started with bottled water. Early on, one of our designers stuck the word 'water' under the 'Thankyou' logo he'd already designed and without exactly planning it, we became known as Thankyou Water from mid-2008 to mid-2013. Since mid-2013, we've simply been called Thankyou.

It's a little awkward when you first meet someone or put a call through, and you tell people you are "from Thankyou" but it sure does strike up a conversation – it's something of a marketer's dream, actually! It's the equivalent of telling someone you're from "Banana". It sounds stupid until one day, like Apple, you become a globally recognised and respected brand.

While it took us three years to sell our first 1 million bottles, from there we quickly grew to sell the second million, then the third and fourth million over the next 12 months. After our launch into 7-Eleven, Australia Post rolled out our product into over 800 of their stores, which meant that our bottled water was now in front of 800,000 people each day in the post office queue.

Our awareness soon began to spike, and this was the point where we were able to finally transition from a volunteer organisation to a sustainable social enterprise that employed a number of staff. While this was a big milestone, it was kind of funny that we had planned for that transition to happen three months into the journey, instead of three years down the track. We started with three paid staff – Jarryd, Justine and myself. We moved from our one-room office into an amazing three-level converted warehouse in Collingwood, thanks to a very generous landlord who helped support us by offering discounted rent.

It was actually a little bit awkward when we moved in because for the first few months, Justine, Jarryd and I had one level each. But we were scaling for growth and over the coming months, we were able to gradually fill more positions. Two years later, we were bursting at the seams in that office with all the desk space taken up by 14 staff.

By financial year 2011, we'd funded over 2000 people gaining access to safe water, but between 2011 and 2013 we grew significantly. By financial year 2013 we were able to fund access to safe water for over 56,000 people, through nearly 4000 water solutions implemented in over 100 projects across 15 countries.

What people *didn't* know is that for around 18 months of those two years, we were working on something bigger – something that Australia and, in fact, the world had never seen before. Everything was kept confidential as we prepared behind the scenes for our next giant leap.

LAST-MINUTE CHANGES SAVE THE DAY

By September 2012, we were ready to offer a hint as to where Thankyou would be heading.

We decided to host our first-ever Thankyou Private Gala. We invited our suppliers, retail partners, distributors, corporate partners, supporters, volunteers and many other people who had helped build Thankyou Water from the ground up. We'd never run an event this big before and we were, as usual, working with a shoestring budget.

We found sponsors, partnered with catering and printing companies and even had the venue donated by a lovely lady in Collingwood, who owned a warehouse-style furniture shop. She was nice enough to say that she'd move all her furniture out and give us the space for the event for free.

Two weeks before the event, with invites sent out and over 200 registered VIP guests, we weren't quite on the same page with our venue. She'd changed her mind and decided she wanted her furniture scattered throughout the entire venue, meaning most of our prepared displays wouldn't be able to make an appearance. Thankfully, a group of guys we'd met through friends of friends offered up their warehouse down the road in Easey Street, Collingwood, and it happened to be one of the coolest warehouses ever. They saved the day.

David Koch, the host of *Sunrise*, flew down from Sydney to host the event at no charge, which blew us away. He wouldn't even let us pay for a cab back to the airport! We had promised guests that there would be great entertainment, but behind the scenes we had a slight issue in that every band we booked kept bailing. Just a few days before the event, we managed to lock in Evermore to play and once again, the day was saved.

While we were experiencing quite a makeshift event behind the scenes, with lots of last-minute saves, the guests fortunately didn't know anything was ever amiss as they strolled into a well-lit warehouse (powered by a generator we hired hours before the event, because the power kept tripping).

We were overwhelmed with the response of our VIPs, who were completely captivated by all the displays, photos and stories from the field, not to mention the amazing catering, which you had to see and sample to believe. That night we launched our television ad, which Channel 9 (and later Channel 7) committed to running for free. We also announced that we'd soon be launching our new tracking system called Track Your Impact.

Just before dessert, we took a moment to thank some of our key partners and then made our big announcement. We shared with the audience that the event wasn't a standard fundraiser or gala, but instead, we were officially launching the next stage of Thankyou.

We explained that we didn't want anyone's money, we just wanted each of them to support the next stage in our journey through their influence. During my speech, I outlined that we were planning to expand from bottled water alone into launching a food range that would fund food programs in developing countries, and body care products that would fund health and hygiene projects. All of our product ranges would come under the brand name 'Thankyou'.

We didn't talk about specific products; all we said was that the products we were planning to launch would be as good as, if not better than, our competitors' and that they would exist to change the world. We knew that if we attempted to sell an average product, people may buy it once due to the cause attached to it, but if it wasn't high quality they would go back to buying the products they actually liked. We also left them with one more piece of information: we would launch in the middle of 2013 in a way that no brand had ever launched before.

LEAPING FROM WATER TO FOOD PRODUCTS...

Global poverty is a complex issue with no simple fix. People write books about it, and then other people write more books about it, stating how the other books didn't even consider a range of other complexities. I'm not an expert but I know that 1 billion people are living in extreme poverty and many are dying from lack of access to basic human rights and conveniences that the developed world takes for granted.

Meanwhile in our country, we spend hundreds of millions, even billions of dollars on everyday products. When we visited our water projects around the world we saw how crucial they were in providing a basic need, but there were other huge issues that needed attention. People required solutions in the areas of food security and health, hygiene and sanitation, just to name a few.

It's one thing to be passionate about championing a cause and making a difference, but doing it through launching a product range that has any chance of succeeding in the fast-moving consumer goods industry in Australia is quite another thing altogether.

I'm sure people may have left our gala event feeling sceptical that we could make the leap from water to other product lines. After all, it's pretty easy to convince the public that we bottle great water, but let's be honest – water is water. The jump to producing food and body care products may have seemed impossible to those who knew what we were planning.

While we had announced our big plans to all of our partners in order to help build momentum, unfortunately, the behind-the-scenes preparations weren't going well. You'd think that because we had some mild success with water, maybe we'd have a bit of a reputation in the industry. We did have a reputation, but it was in beverages, not food, which was where we planned to launch next.

At the end of one of our very first meetings with a massive food manufacturer, the guy literally told us to come back when we were serious.

That said, he wasn't the first to tell us that we had no idea what we were getting ourselves into. We spoke to many experienced people in the industry and the information and the feedback we received was pretty depressing. We were once told just "stick to our knitting", to which I may have responded back in humour and frustration, "But we don't knit."

We were making a big leap from water to food, so to help make it possible we enlisted Callum Hann. Callum had won *MasterChef Australia All Stars*, written cookbooks and was running his own cooking school, Sprout. Just like us, Callum was young and optimistic enough to believe that we could actually pull our plan off.

We invited him to join our team as our CTO, or Chief Taste Officer. The role wasn't just for show, because the reality was that we knew how to make water, but we had no idea how to make food! We put Callum in charge of developing, alongside our team and suppliers, a food range that would give competitors a serious run for their money. We've joked in the past that if we ever wrote a book, the story of the day we pitched to Callum was always going to make it in.

Callum wouldn't like me to say this, but the truth is that he's a pretty big deal. There have been a lot of *MasterChef* television seasons in Australia and while he came runner-up in the second season, he later came back on the *All Stars* season and took out the top prize. He may fight me on playing up his reputation, but I clearly remember being out for lunch with him when two girls stopped and stared, and then blurted out, "Oh my gosh, are you Callum from *MasterChef*?"

We found out he was going to be in Melbourne, so we decided to invite him to our office. All he knew was that we wanted to meet up and pitch an idea to him. I picked him up from his hotel and he was telling me in the car that he was in town to judge a muesli bar company's new flavour competition. Not only was he judging, but they had also flown him over and put him up in a hotel.

As we drove to the office I asked him a lot of questions about his involvement with this muesli bar company and I'm sure he was wondering what was with my fascination with muesli bars. Thankfully, I was able to figure out from the conversation that he wasn't under contract with this particular company and neither did he have any ongoing commitment to them.

That was really handy because 20 minutes later, Justine, Jarryd and I were in our boardroom with Callum, inviting him to come on board and help develop a market-leading product range that would include muesli bars, muesli, cluster oats and quick oats.

Callum was speechless for a moment. Then he said quietly, "This will *only* work if the products are actually amazing." He loved the idea that we could use food, which he was passionate about, to help solve the global food crisis but like us, he knew that at the end of the day it would all come down to quality and taste. Within a short period of time, Callum was officially part of the team.

Callum worked with our team and some of Australia's leading suppliers to develop an incredible range of products. We developed mueslis with super foods, real fruit and less sugar than other brands on the market. We couldn't believe that our Nut Bar ended up stacking up better; from a nutritional perspective, when compared to some of the 'healthy bars' that are meant to help you watch your weight – and the best part is that ours actually tasted good.

We worked hard to keep all manufacturing in Australia because we believe in supporting the Australian economy while at the same time helping people in need around the world.

... AND LAUNCHING INTO BODY CARE

While the food range was getting under way, we were also developing the body care products, specifically hand wash and hand lotion. By caring for their bodies in purchasing this range, customers would be able to fund access to hygiene and sanitation programs for people in need.

These products essentially funded the software behind the hardware (being the water projects). The reality is that there is not much point drinking clean water when you have dirty hands; we've since expanded the funding into latrines and other components of sanitation.

The development of this range was absolutely fascinating. We wanted to bring consumers a premium product that contained plant-derived ingredients at an everyday price. There were already many other brands that offered a similar natural and premium product, but they came with a price tag of $30 to $50. Because we were positioning our range to appeal to everyday Australians we knew we needed to deliver the same quality, but hit an everyday affordable price point of no more than $7 to $10. During our first meetings with potential manufacturers, we talked about these premium brands and received some pretty honest responses from experts in the industry – many suggesting that "it's all in the marketing".

We were quite surprised to discover that many of these incredibly expensive bottles of hand wash were in fact just that – hand wash. There was nothing all that special about them. They were not as expensive to produce as you might imagine, but by setting their pricing at a high premium, consumers were under the impression that they were getting a very high-quality product – when in fact they were just getting a good product (no arguments there) with excellent marketing, celebrity endorsements and in some cases, well-located retail outlets.

In our case, we knew we were targeting a consumer who wanted a quality and premium product at an affordable price. So, we set out on a journey to create this affordable luxury product. Working with one of Australia's leading chemists, a world-leading fragrance house and a local, experienced supplier, we put together an initial range of hand wash and hand lotion. As I've said before, with the right team of people, anything is possible.

CREATING PROOF OF IMPACT

While developing these product ranges, we also developed our Track Your Impact 2.0 system. We'd done a soft launch for the system in 2012 with our water products but we were developing it further, with the idea being that every product has its own individual tracker code.

The two biggest questions most people have when it comes to supporting a cause are, where does the money really go, and do I even make an impact? We've developed Track Your Impact to help answer these questions.

Every single Thankyou product has a unique code (or 'Tracker ID') on the label and these days we have millions of codes on the market at any one time. Each code is assigned to a specific part of a specific project. Consumers can enter their unique code into our website and using GPS coordinates, they can zoom in on Google Maps to see the exact project that their product is assigned to fund. In some cases, you can literally see the roofs in the community your Thankyou product is assigned to assist. And if you sign in through Facebook or Gmail it allows your profile to be stored, so we can help you track your accumulated impact over time.

It's a huge process that takes a large amount of collaboration with everyone involved, from suppliers through to our dedicated field partners. But we feel that the level of detail we give consumers via Track Your Impact is the same level of reporting that a high net worth donor would usually receive from a large charity – we just make it available for any person who buys one of our products, even if they do so just once.

Here's the thing: we don't feel that what's been achieved with Track Your Impact is hugely remarkable. We've assigned a code from a product to a specific project, to help connect you with the fact that every product makes an impact. It's a step in the right direction, but it's what comes next that really helps me sleep at night.

You see, once a project is complete (this can be up to 12 months after a customer has 'tracked'), we'll email everyone who signed up to track their impact with a final field report, including photographic proof (complete with GPS coordinates) of the project their product was assigned to fund.

Why go to this much effort?

It's because we want to ensure everyone – from those in our team, to the partners we work with – is always on the same page. In the early days, our team turned up once to visit some wells we'd funded and when we got there, the wells weren't there. They didn't exist.

But the bigger issue for us wasn't the potential PR disaster, it was the fact that we thought we had established – and had provided funding for – access to safe water for this community in Kenya.

We could see with our own eyes that they didn't have it. After some frantic phone calls with our project partners, we were assured it was a matter of miscommunication and when we re-visited the site 12 months later, we were pleased to find the works had been completed.

These types of stories are riddled across various parts of the world where development projects take place. With Track Your Impact, everyone is tied to an extra layer of accountability. Our field app captures the GPS coordinates of where the photographic proof of the project is taken, allowing our team to crosscheck all programs and then report back to our customers.

Track Your Impact has become a pillar of Thankyou. The team that has worked on bringing it to life (and continue to develop it) are insanely smart people. In fact, most times when I walk past their computers, it looks like the Matrix and I can't even tell if they are actually working or not. But the system works, so they must be doing something right!

Track Your Impact aside, it's hard to explain just how much work and resources were required to move from our water bottles to having three product ranges, and in such a short period of time as well. On top of the incredible amount of effort it took to develop new products, we had to roll out our rebranding strategy, fresh marketing campaigns and a new website – plus we had the small challenge of funding it all.

THAT ANNOYING AND EVER-PRESENT DETAIL: MONEY

We needed a large sum of money to get these new products off the ground. Purely from a manufacturing and launch strategy point of view, the figures were staggering to us, as the initial estimates were upwards of $800,000.

This amount was just the initial seed money we needed to prepare the product for full commercial production, and cover our launch. We worked out that with a lot of crunching the numbers, we could pull it off for around half of that amount, at $400,000.

The challenge we had was that although Thankyou Water was going well, we didn't have a lazy half-million sitting in our accounts. While Thankyou Water as a business was generating profits, those profits were designed to fund water projects, not to fund blue-sky business developments.

With all of our commitments to our projects overseas, the staff we needed to manage our current business, plus the time we were investing into developing the new range, we just couldn't find that kind of capital. About four months before our forecasted launch in July, I was sitting down with one of our financial advisors and he asked, "How are you going with raising capital?", referring to the $400,000 that he knew we needed.

Our plan had been to raise about $200,000 in social investment, via a very low interest loan, and $200,000 in donated funds. My answer was simple, if a little disappointing. "We've had $1000 come in," I said. I wasn't even being funny.

After 12 months of meetings with some seriously wealthy people, trying to convince them that we were worth giving to, all that we had been able to raise was $1000, which was generously donated by two of Justine's former bosses. When they gave it to us there was a note attached that said, "We know it's only small, but we wanted to support you." Little did they know that their kind donation was the sum total of every donation we had physically received to date for the new products and launch!

We'd also been working with someone else, who was close to committing $100,000 in a low interest social loan, but we hadn't signed off on the paperwork yet.

Our financial advisor's reaction, as you could imagine, was surprise mixed with concern. Like us, he's a positive dreamer – but he knew as well as I did that the reality facing us was quite shocking. The thought of postponing the launch was a real possibility. You might be wondering how you develop an incredible product range when you actually don't have the money. Here's the thing: all of our suppliers had actually covered all of our R&D costs because they wanted our business.

In our initial pitch meetings, we had told them, "This is going to change the game in the market and you wouldn't want to miss out." We were not being unethical, because it's normal practice for manufacturers to invest in initial R&D, but they are careful who they work with and invest in. From this point, we needed to take the developed product to full production phase, which is where we had to start tipping in some serious money.

In that meeting with our financial advisor, I said something that really sums up the entire philosophy of Thankyou. Some call it boldness, some call it stupidity, but I call it faith. "The launch is going ahead in July," I said, "and it's going to be exciting to see where the money comes from." Like I read in that book years earlier, "If the idea is good enough, the money will come."

The different people I had met with about our funding requirements had a lot of experience and a lot of money, but they just weren't getting our vision. I'd show them the products, which they liked, and some of them even got to hear our grand launch plans, but that is where we lost most of them because we were ultimately banking on a very big 'if'.

In Australia, our two major supermarkets, Coles and Woolworths, comprise around 70 per cent of the grocery market. It's unlike any other global retail market, and we are one of the only countries in the world where a retail duopoly exists in the supermarket space.

To make the whole exercise financially viable and sustainable, we had to (at a very minimum) get one of them on board. We knew that if we landed both of them, it would really take off. There are other great retailers and avenues to explore in Australia, but the majority of new product sales flows from these two supermarket giants, which allows you to produce the product at a competitive price to then sell via other smaller retailers.

To complicate things a little further, we had been in business for five years and neither Coles nor Woolworths had accepted our water product. Nearly all of our potential donors and social investors couldn't see how, after half a decade of unsuccessful attempts to get Thankyou Water into either of the two major supermarkets, we were going to get over 16 new products ranged in one shot.

The suggestion we often heard was to just try them one at a time, which would mean less money upfront and therefore less risk. At this point in the conversation, I thought that telling them our secret grand plan (which I'll share with you shortly) would get them excited about our vision – but it only made them more concerned.

In hindsight, I can understand their apprehension. Because our secret grand plan was a huge risk.

NO PLAN B

When people asked what our plan B was if the two major supermarkets didn't range our new product, the only answer I could give them was, "A good plan A doesn't have a plan B."

I'm sure that's a line from a movie and I can imagine that some people mistook it for total incompetence or complete arrogance. But the fact was, we had only developed products with the largest manufacturers in the country, so that we could handle production once we got into the supermarkets. There *was* no plan B. At all. Some of these suppliers had minimum run sizes of four tonnes – just under 90,000 units in some cases – which meant we couldn't start small. We *had* to start big.

We didn't see it as an option to find a small factory, run a couple of pallets of product and spend the next 5 to 10 years trying to build the brand until one day, hopefully, the supermarkets would take the product. In our minds, people are living in extreme poverty *today* and need people to partner with them *now*, not in 10 years. Ultimately, we felt it was go hard or go home.

The next four months comprised the craziest period of our entire lives – which is saying something, because you know by now how chaotic the previous four years had been! We were finalising the development of 16 different products across three different ranges and this didn't just mean developing the concept; it involved the entire process of getting them ready for a mass-market launch.

Just getting all of the legal elements of packaging correct nearly killed us, and then there were the constant hiccups along the way that we didn't expect. We nearly ditched the entire body care range two weeks before launch after one of our fragrance houses majorly messed us around, but we were able to make it happen, thanks to the support of a new world-class fragrance house that came to the rescue at the eleventh hour.

Suppliers kept asking when our first meeting was with the supermarkets, to which we said July. They were quite concerned that we hadn't already met with them, since usually the idea is to be in contact with them while developing the products.

It was incredibly difficult getting our suppliers to work to our deadlines because they kept saying, "After your first meeting, even if it goes really well, you'd be lucky to have product on the shelf within 12 to 18 months." But we always pushed back, promising them that after the meeting, "they will order fast".

Then there was the fact that our meeting was scheduled for July, which was not during their 'range review' period – typically the only time supermarkets range new products.

We hadn't told any of our suppliers our secret grand plans due to their confidential nature – and also because we knew they'd probably freak out. We just kept stressing to suppliers that we could be getting orders in August (three or four weeks after our meeting), so they had to be ready or else we'd have to take our business elsewhere. It's always tough when you have no experience dealing with the supermarkets, and you're trying to convince people who have 10 or 20 years in the game, that you know what you're doing.

On top of this, we had committed to building the biggest website we'd ever built, and we were working with project partners to line up food and hygiene and sanitation projects, because those agreements take months to set in place. Plus, we were developing the biggest marketing launch we'd ever attempted, and – oh, that's right – there was still the money thing.

A few weeks before our scheduled July launch, we had an amazing couple sit down with us in our office. They had watched our journey and they were two of many people who we had met with about finance. Deep down, they believed wholeheartedly in our vision and that we had what it would take to pull this off.

To our great relief and shock, they told us that they would be giving us $100,000 as a donation, plus an additional $100,000 low-interest social loan. We were speechless and of course, beyond grateful.

Another young guy and his family then signed off on a similar $100,000 loan; he and his wife had been fans of the brand for a very long time and in fact, I was asked to speak at his MBA class, after they did a project and raised a few thousand dollars for us. We were so grateful. You never know what seemingly brief connections can grow into.

Following this, we received news from another group who we'd been in discussions with that they would be donating $80,000. What amazed me about these three groups was that they were giving us finance with no strings attached; they didn't require being on our board or having any control of how we ran Thankyou. They didn't even want public recognition and said they'd prefer to give privately.

With $381,000 behind us ($200,000 worth of low-interest social loans and $181,000 in donated finance), we were ready to go. We could cover all of the big costs involved in getting our new products ready for mass production. We could fund the grand launch plan that we had developed and we would have enough left to help our cash flow position, as we went from a really small company to a really big one overnight… If it all went to plan.

After 18 months of work, we'd developed 16 new products, raised the capital needed to produce them, had warehouses full of raw materials ready to take the products to mass market, had signed agreements with project partners overseas who were now awaiting funding, had developed a website that basically was six websites combined into one, had developed Track Your Impact 2.0, *and* we'd finished our preparations for a world-first product launch strategy… one that put the entire reputation of our organisation, and even our personal reputations as directors, on the line.

Everything hinged on this one secret and grand plan and we were fully aware that it could most definitely fail. The slightly scary part was that failure wouldn't just mean a year and a half's work wasted. We knew our idea was so crazy that if it didn't work, we'd be the laughing stock of the industry and there was a chance that we would never be taken seriously again.

In other words: if this flopped, it could be all over for us.

But the one question that kept us going in the months leading up to our grand launch, during the many sleepless nights leading up to July 17, 2013, was this: "What if this *does* work?"

SOME THOUGHTS TO TAKE AWAY:

ONE. When building your dream, patience and longevity are key. We always knew that Thankyou was about more than just water, but we also knew we had to start small and scale over time.

TWO. People might question or discredit your ability to innovate, but don't let discouragement or criticism stop you from taking that next step forwards if you believe deep down that it's the right move.

THREE. Sometimes to be remarkable you have to put in a lot of extra work. Over the years, we've had a lot of people tell us that the amount of effort we put into Track Your Impact could (and should) be applied to something else to grow the business. But it's become a pillar of our organisation and it's what connects our customers to impact – so the hard work is more than worth it.

FOUR. Some of the most disruptive and successful organisations in our world began with a risky idea. Always ask, "What if it works?" – even when everyone around you is asking, "What if it doesn't?"

FIVE. Don't quote me on this (I'm clearly not a financial advisor) but if an idea is good enough, the money will come!

CHAPTER 1.8
The Campaign That Changed It All

This particular day in the Thankyou office began like no other.

The morning we launched our secret grand plan, at 8.30am on Wednesday July 17, 2013, our team *should* have been calmly gathered around the television.

We were minutes away from seeing our biggest TV feature to date run on *Sunrise*, which was set to air at 8.45am. The story would announce to the public that we were no longer Thankyou Water, that we were rebranding to simply Thankyou and that we were also launching 16 further products across our new food and body care ranges. Most importantly, it would announce our campaign launch.

The minute the campaign launched, we needed people to rush to our website to watch the launch video and share it across social media. Why? Because our campaign relied fully on the support of the public and the video gave a clear call to action to the people watching it.

Fortunately from previous experience, we knew that this segment would attract tens of thousands of visitors to our website seconds after it went to air, which is exactly what we needed. Our new website (the one that we'd spent nearly 12 months working on) was up for the challenge... until it wasn't.

Two days prior to the launch, the site crashed for "unknown reasons". Our web guy Simon was up all night trouble-shooting and luckily, he fixed it just in time.

But the launch video – the focus of the entire campaign – wouldn't upload properly. The guys had pulled all-nighters to get it ready but the video still wasn't uploading to our YouTube account quickly enough.

At 8.15am, our team was in major panic mode – you could see the stress on all of our faces. We'd prepared for this moment for 18 months, and it felt like it was about to fall apart because of technical difficulties to do with a video upload! You can understand now why we weren't feeling very calm… Just minutes before our segment went to air on *Sunrise*, a YouTube notification arrived to confirm that the video was uploaded and ready to go live. You really couldn't cut it any finer!

Later that day our creative designer Wesley informed Justine that, just to top it all off, our emails had gone down too. Wesley hadn't told us at the time as he didn't want to add to our stress; Simon, our web developer, had managed to fix it a few minutes before launch.

The launch video we'd prepared wasn't your average video clip. Justine was leading the campaign and when she and her creative team shared the idea for the clip with me I liked it – until I realised what I had to do. You see, the creative team had gone to town and my role was simple: I had the fun task of memorising the six-and-a-half-minute script and articulating it clearly to the camera, while also attempting to perfectly time my words with the corresponding actions… as we moved backwards through a 200m set, filming the entire clip in just one take!

Many social media experts say that for an online viral video to be successful, it shouldn't be longer than two to three minutes. There was no way we could fit everything we wanted to into that time, so we decided to take a gamble and hope that our longer video length wouldn't put people off.

During the concept stage, it sounded like a great idea to shoot a video in one take but as it turns out, the practicalities of actually implementing that concept are complicated, to say the least. Later on, marketing experts estimated that it "would have cost over $100,000 to make" our video, and "it would have taken at least a week to film". In reality, we invested about $8000 and spent just one day filming because we figured that was plenty of time.

None of us, including our videographer/creative genius, Daniel, had attempted a video like this before. As usual, we'd underestimated the project but we were forced to nail it in the timeframe we had with the very limited budget we possessed. We had an incredible team on board that day, which meant that somehow, we managed to get the job done.

THE MAKE OR BREAK MOMENT

Back to the launch morning. With our website up and running and our launch video ready (and unbeknownst to us, our emails back on track), our team watched in awe at 8.45am as *Sunrise* aired one of the best segments on Thankyou we had ever seen.

They spoke about our journey as Thankyou Water and then introduced our new food and body care ranges. Then, they announced the launch of our biggest campaign yet – The Coles and Woolworths Campaign – and that we had booked meetings with the supermarkets to present our entire range to them in two weeks' time.

At this stage, we had created the products and launched the range, but we still had no national distribution deal. Getting ranged by at least one of the two big supermarket chains was essential to our success.

Sunrise finished the segment by asking Australians to show their support by jumping onto Coles' and Woolworths' Facebook pages, and posting a video or even just a written comment to say: "If you stocked the Thankyou range, I would buy it." It was the same concept we'd used with 7-Eleven but on a much, much bigger scale; this time, we had the two biggest and most competitive retailers in Australia in our sights.

Our website had a banner designed that read, "The Coles and Woolworths Campaign". People said to us, "You can't put Australia's two largest supermarkets – who hate each other – in the same sentence." Our creative team didn't find it too hard though; they just wrote it.

Naturally, our team clicked onto Coles' and Woolworths' Facebook pages straight after the segment and in seconds, hundreds of posts had appeared in favour of our products. In fact, we couldn't scroll down fast enough to see the new entries appear. The views of our YouTube launch video were rising in the hundreds within moments of the launch.

Our Facebook post of the video had hundreds of shares and our own Facebook page was exploding with support for the new products and campaign (you can check out the clip on our YouTube channel, as it summarises the incredible journey we had taken over the five years since launching).

In the 30 minutes after the campaign launched, my phone lit up constantly with text messages of support. It wasn't long before a number I didn't recognise called and I can't quite explain it, but I had a bad feeling about this one. I didn't answer. I checked my messages and it was a buyer from one of the supermarkets. I listened to the voicemail message and he was extremely upset. He expressed a few thoughts about unprofessionalism and common courtesy. My heart was racing as I listened to him talk, but I knew that now wasn't the time to call him back – we had a campaign to run. We had to prove to these supermarkets how big this was and at this point, it consisted of one media story and a few hundred Facebook messages. They had no idea what else was coming.

As the morning went on, our team and their friends and family shared the video through all, and I mean all, of their networks. We'd lined up as many people as we could to help seed the video in as many different blogs, forums and social media channels as possible. We needed the video to get a huge amount of views over the next few days. In fact, this momentum had to continue for the next 14 days or it wouldn't work – the supermarkets would see the campaign as just a bit of hype and not the true consumer movement we believed it was.

At about midday, the buyer called again and once again, I let it ring to message bank. When I checked the message it was the same guy, but let's just say he had a very different tone to his previous message. He was sounding much more positive and this time, he actually said he was looking forward to our meeting!

This was a good sign that the campaign was working, because we'd obviously grabbed the attention of a few people in the organisation. I called back and we had a brief but positive chat. He wanted to move the meeting forward from the original date of Tuesday (in two weeks' time) – when we had both the Coles and Woolworths meetings booked – to the very next day. We had anticipated that either supermarket might try one of two things: to jump the gun on the other one, or attempt to shut the campaign down. Both outcomes could be achieved by calling an early meeting.

We knew the importance of momentum and we were not prepared to meet until we believed we'd shown them the power of the consumer movement behind the brand. We told him that we could move the meeting forward three days, from the planned date of Tuesday to the Friday before. It was a risk, because we had to face the prospect of not being able to maintain the momentum for two weeks, but we had a plan and we had to stick to it.

As a side note, it was interesting to see how each supermarket reacted. One was quick to communicate and very friendly. The other gave us no acknowledgement during the first few days, and didn't even respond to the information packs that we sent through to their media team. It wasn't until 9.30am seven days *after* we launched that we heard from them. I'll explain further on why that was such a significant moment.

MONITORING THE MEDIA STORM (AND MANAGING THE HATERS)

The media coverage of our unorthodox launch was intense, to say the least. Many marketing media publications and trade magazines picked up the campaign, which helped distribute our story to the entire fast-moving consumer goods industry. We'd set a goal to reach 10,000 views of the video by the end of the campaign, as our best-performing video in our five-year history to that point had received 10,000 views, so that was our benchmark. By the end of day one, we were already approaching that goal.

By day two, we were engaged in a steady stream of media interviews; newspapers, radio, blogs, the list went on. Over the entire campaign we appeared in more than 90 mainstream media features, which weren't just little plugs, but decent-sized articles – including a three-page spread in *BRW*.

One entire level in our office was converted into a buzzing press office headed up by Sarah, who had come to us from working at one of the big car manufacturers, joining Thankyou not long after we landed 7-Eleven Australia. She had not only played a huge role in helping Justine in the million things that had to be done in the lead up, but she was now running a PR campaign of epic proportions.

Our new pro bono PR agency at the time, Click PR (now known as Sling & Stone), even sent in a full-time senior executive to assist our team during the campaign. It was a crazy time with all hands on deck and very little sleep – but we were too focused on our end goal to let something as insignificant as exhaustion get in the way!

Many of the journalists that interviewed me during this period said things like, "You guys are nuts" or, "Do you realise you're backing the two biggest retailers into a corner; they are not going to like you very much!" One even asked me, live on radio, "Can you even do this?!" to which I responded, "I suppose we'll find out at the meeting!"

However, just as happened with our earlier 7-Eleven campaign, people got behind us in incredibly creative ways. And this time around it went to a whole new level. Entire schools supported us; people wrote full-length songs; we had over a dozen celebrities add their weight by recording videos and some of them even encouraged their online networks to get behind the campaign.

The list of well-known supporters included Andrew Gaze, Jules Lund, Chrissie Swan, Kate Peck, Keiynan Lonsdale, Peter Helliar, Dean Geyer, Becca Tobin, Tim Costello, Rebecca Morse, Dylan Lewis, Poh Ling Yeow, Ash London, Scott Tweedie and a DJ with a pretty epic following called tyDi.

What you have to remember is that this didn't happen in just one day. It rolled out over two weeks, which made it even more remarkable and scary. We had team members monitoring how the campaign was tracking on social media and there were a couple of moments where the rate of posts dropped slightly, which was scary, because there was a chance that they could stop altogether. But then it would pick up again, and we'd all exhale in a collective sigh of relief.

Throughout that two-week period, as I mentioned, our team didn't get a whole lot of sleep. In between generating media and doing interviews, we were responding to emails and posts on social media while also providing the public with enough information to win their support of the products – which were technically not even real products yet, because they weren't available for purchase! Every day, we'd wake up to see the video had hit another 5000 or 10,000 views, until finally it reached almost 80,000 views by the end of the campaign. The whole process was exciting, humbling and nerve-wracking, and I don't think our individual hearts stopped racing for any significant period of time during the entire two weeks.

Then, as to be expected, along came the haters. By haters, I mean the people who were making all types of factually incorrect statements and voicing vicious rumours about our organisation. Some of them appeared early on in the campaign, but by week two they'd unfortunately increased in numbers.

We were expecting to attract some criticism after launching such a unique campaign.

When the haters' comments started popping up on social media, we noted with interest that many of these people's Facebook accounts had been created the same day as, or very soon after, the launch date of our campaign (and funnily enough, they had no friends). This told us that they probably were not who they seemed to be. Were they competitors, supermarkets, or just kids who had nothing better to do? It was impossible to tell, but it was clear that they were determined to stop us from progressing.

In some instances, these negative accounts would spend hours commenting back to every person who showed their support for the campaign. This caused some supporters to question us, which meant we had to be on the ball at all times to combat the comments and ensure people weren't misled.

We even had a call from a very angry father who couldn't be calmed down by any of the team. I took the call and listened as he explained that his daughter had gotten behind the campaign in good faith, one of her school friends (whose dad reportedly worked for one of the supermarkets) said that it was all a big marketing set-up, and that we were in cahoots with the retailers. He was convinced that the supermarkets had secretly funded us and it took me a good 20 minutes to calm him down and thank him for his daughter's support.

Even more painful to combat were the personal comments people made on our YouTube channel and Facebook page. They attacked everything from the clothes we were wearing in the video through to our motives. After a while, Justine told me that I wasn't allowed to view the Facebook comments and asked everyone on our team, except for the people who were in charge of responding, to try not to look.

When you've spent a good part of your life building something for the sole purpose of helping others, it can be discouraging to watch people rip into it. But, we had to mentally prepare for the two biggest meetings of our lives while keeping the momentum of the campaign going, which meant that we couldn't let the uninformed and irrational haters bring us down.

Interestingly, the comments made by these people often strengthened our support. We watched as many people in our community rallied and went into bat for us by responding positively to negative comments. I actually think in hindsight that some of the haters helped fuel the video being shared, which then helped drive more support for our cause.

TWO HELICOPTERS, A BABY AND A COUPLE OF GIANT SIGNS

During the planning stage, we'd known that we needed to find a way to execute our campaign offline as well as online. We figured that the supermarkets' corporate affairs and media teams would be well aware of what we were doing, but we needed to somehow make sure the rest of their team were engaged. So, it was time for the cherry on top of the campaign sundae – a stunt that would get the attention of the supermarkets and the wider public. We'd spent weeks preparing for this and due to rain and wind, the stunt had been postponed for three consecutive days in a row. At 4am on a Tuesday morning, we attempted to stage it for a fourth time.

I was picked up by Jess, my PA at the time, and we made our way to the launch site where it would all kick off. Sarah and her team had lined up the best media run we'd ever had, with producers from all major TV news, radio and newspaper outlets having been given an embargoed media call out the night before.

They were all excited, although one producer did say at one point, "You better pray that baby isn't born." In the early hours of the same morning, "that baby" was indeed born – that baby being Prince George. You guessed it; we lost most of our media spots.

However, that didn't stop us from pressing on with the task at hand. The logistics of the stunt involved three helicopters, three helicopter pilots and five camera and video operators – spread across Melbourne and Sydney. Jess and I didn't say a lot as we drank our iced coffees on the way to the airport, we'd heard the news of the birth of Prince George and were watching rain fall on the windscreen. It wasn't heavy rain, but it needed to stop in the next half hour or our plan would be postponed – again.

We got to the airport and the Melbourne camera crew and helicopter people were preparing for take off. They were excited because they'd been watching the campaign and couldn't believe what we were about to do. While no one seemed too concerned about the weather, I can tell you that it was a far cry from our vision of a blue-sky day.

By 8am we were ready to go. I watched as the helicopter took off from the ground carrying a 10,000 square foot sign (30m x 30m). The sign was black with bold white and red writing that read: "Dear Coles, Thank you for changing the world (if you say yes)", followed by our web address. At the same time we had a helicopter taking off in Sydney with a sign saying: "Hi Woolworths, Together we can change the world (if you say yes)".

Literally minutes before launch, the rain turned to drizzle and not long after, it stopped altogether.

Finally we had reached the moment: this was real, this was happening and once I was standing under the sign, I couldn't believe how big 10,000 square feet actually was.

The idea behind this crazy stunt all began when, in one of our creative meetings, we talked about holding a sign out the front of the supermarkets' head offices during the campaign. We figured their security would just come and kick us out before the sign had a chance to make any impact, and as you know by now, we like to dream big at Thankyou.

Then someone had the idea to hang the sign from a helicopter that would fly above their head offices, and we knew we were onto a winner. Of course, we didn't have any money to do it, so we pitched the bold idea to the helicopter companies to donate their time (they did) and also arrange a donor to pay for the sign (they did that, too).

The helicopters flew up the freeways during peak hour traffic and around each head office for about 25 minutes. A second helicopter followed one of them to film it and we had photographers and videographers set up at landmark points to film the stunt for media and social media.

WHAT DIFFERENCE WOULD A COUPLE OF DAYS MAKE?

Near the end of the stunt, my phone rang. It was the other supermarket that hadn't contacted us yet. It looked like our little 'fly by' had worked. "I hear we have a meeting booked for next week," he said. Out of courtesy, I told him that the other supermarket had moved their meeting forwards to this Friday and offered them the same opportunity to meet that day, as we didn't want to favour either supermarket in particular.

He was pretty straight to the point and replied, "It's not like anything is going to happen between a Friday and a Tuesday, so there's no need – we'll see you Tuesday." It was a fair point. Products take months, sometimes even years, to secure ranging in a supermarket, so what difference would a couple of days make?

By this point we'd walked an interesting journey with some of our key stakeholders. Our suppliers who had developed products with us only found out about our plans the night before launch. They all work closely with the supermarkets on other products and I wanted them to be able to say honestly that they didn't know anything about it, if the situation turned sour and the supermarkets questioned them about their involvement with us.

When I put that call through the night before launch to tell our suppliers, the responses were a mix of speechlessness, excitement and concern – but it was too late for anyone's opinion to stop the launch. They had played their role, to make great products, and now it was our turn to get the products ranged.

Many of the industry experts we'd spoken to throughout the campaign liked what we were trying to achieve, but just didn't believe it would work. Belief is a powerful thing and our team had believed for over a year and a half that we could pull this off. This is an important point, because just days before our first meeting with the first supermarket, we had to draw on our reserves of self-belief in a big way.

I'm not sure what you were like at school, but personally, if an assignment was due on a certain day, I was usually up until very late the night before and probably the next morning working on it. There is something about a deadline that increases my productivity and effectiveness. So there

I was, two nights before our big presentation… and I hadn't yet started working on the pitch. I knew what we wanted to say, I just hadn't actually put it together yet.

On this particular night I was in Coffs Harbour – two plane rides from home – as I had committed to speaking at a youth event the next day. I spent that night on the phone to a range of different mentors. We talked about all the possible ways the meeting could go and discussed strategies to make sure we had all bases covered. The next day after speaking at the event, I flew back to Melbourne and spent the afternoon and evening working on my 50-slide PowerPoint pitch. I completed it at 3am and sent it to Jan-Lee, our creative designer, who had the task of getting it ready by 6am for the big pitch that day.

After finishing that last minute presentation prep (at 3am), I should have gone straight to sleep to get a couple of hours' rest. But I didn't; instead I opened my laptop and clicked onto Coles' and Woolworths' Facebook pages. I began trawling through the posts. I had spent the last week running from media interviews to meetings and speaking engagements, while also dealing with various issues and preparing for our pitches, which meant I hadn't actually watched or read many of the posts by our fans.

What should have been only a few minutes on Facebook turned into an hour of browsing as I watched video after video and read post after post. It was one of the most humbling moments I've experienced in our entire journey. To see thousands of people I'd never met go to such huge efforts to back our campaign, combined with lack of sleep and probably extreme exhaustion, brought me to tears.

So far, this campaign had exceeded all of our expectations.

While it may have appeared that we were simply attempting some sort of ambush marketing, our idea with this campaign was much bigger than just getting the products stocked on the shelves at the supermarkets. We knew that the win wasn't just about getting the product ranged: it was (and is) having the product actually *sell*.

We needed to raise national awareness to get our products moving off the shelves quickly enough for the supermarkets to keep ranging them. That sort of awareness is where the 'millions of dollars in marketing budgets' comes in handy. Clearly, we didn't have millions of dollars so this campaign was our plan of attack. It was designed to raise massive awareness and get people to pre-commit to purchasing, which was the closest we could possibly get to proving that our products might sell.

There was no doubt that we had put it all on the line – including our brand and personal reputations. Over those two weeks, everyone who didn't previously know about us in the industry now knew about us, and if we weren't successful, we knew it would be tough to recover from it. I'm not even sure how you'd attempt to rebuild a relationship with the supermarkets (not to mention our suppliers) if this failed.

OUR FIRST SUPERMARKET MEETING

On the morning of our pitch to the first supermarket, I woke up less than two hours after I'd fallen asleep. Having spent most of the night completing my presentation and watching campaign videos, through some miraculous act of God I actually woke up with energy.

That morning, Jarryd, Justine and I headed off to the meeting of a lifetime. The surreal feeling I had when driving towards that appointment is hard to explain. With adrenaline pumping through every cell of our beings, we walked through those head office doors. I could have been reading into things, but it felt like we were getting a lot of looks from people in the waiting room. I figured it was either the skinny jeans and blazer combo I was wearing (standard for me, but not your typical corporate get up) or that maybe, just maybe, they'd seen the campaign video.

Our contact walked us through the office and into the meeting room. As we walked up the stairs and through the corridors, I couldn't help but notice the sheer volume of floor-to-ceiling glass that covered every floor. I realised that virtually all of their head office employees – all several thousand of them – would have seen our helicopter fly by.

We walked into a boardroom to be greeted by some of their team who were, to our relief, smiling. We met people from all different parts of the business and there were some high-level executives in the room. They opened with, "Well, you've got our attention," and I jumped into our presentation as quickly as I could, trying to gauge their reaction as I spoke.

A few times, they cut in to ask some crucial questions and we had the opportunity to explain why we ran the campaign the way we did – particularly the fact that, while it may have appeared to be an ambush, our plan was simply to show them what we wanted to accomplish and to set them up with the perfect opportunity to make a difference and be loved for it.

Something I often have to remind myself in these types of meetings is that you're meeting with *real people*. You can hear all sorts of scary stories about retailers or CEOs or specific organisations, but when you're sitting at the same table, you realise that at the end of the day, they are just people like you and me.

Towards the end of the presentation, I was feeling good. These guys seemed to love what we were doing as much as we did and they said some encouraging things like, "You did what you had to do to stand out in a crowded market and we love that."

I then clicked over to my final slide – it was one that we were really divided on as a team. It was titled 'Exclusivity'. Almost everyone we had spoken to had said that both of the supermarkets would push for exclusivity and asked what our strategy would be to deal with that. To be honest, we'd been unsure about what to do.

We saw the benefit of being exclusive to one supermarket and having them really push our brand and give us marketing support. But we saw the bigger benefit of being in both supermarkets and having access to the 'other half' of the Australian population.

That said, we figured we better at least open the discussion. When I put the slide up, one of their senior executives spoke before I had a chance to open my mouth. The three of us will never forget his words, because they quite possibly changed the growth and success of Thankyou as it stands today.

"I wouldn't be talking about that if I were you," he said, adding that what we were doing was "bigger than one supermarket". "The bigger you are, the bigger the impact you'll make," he concluded. "If we do decide to range the products, it wouldn't be based on exclusivity, it will be based on the merit of your products and your organisation, so let's take that off the table."

I couldn't believe what I was hearing. We were not sitting with opportunists; they look for exclusivity and leverage. We were sitting opposite genuine potential partners! I finished by saying, "Well, let's just go back one slide and forget we even mentioned the 'E' word." After a few more questions, the meeting ended.

It was a relief to finish what had felt like a marathon. We left their head office almost too exhausted to think about how the meeting had gone, let alone discuss it. That afternoon, the three of us left work at about 4pm. Justine and I went straight to the movies to see the new Hugh Jackman film, *Wolverine* – we needed to do something to switch off. At 5pm we sat down with our popcorn and right as the first scene opened, my phone began to ring.

I wasn't sure if I recognised the number or not but I had that feeling, that gut feeling, that I should answer the call. Should we have really been in a movie straight after a meeting this big? I ran up the back of the cinema and out the door and took the call. It was the supermarket we'd met with that morning and I was on loudspeaker with more than one person; they asked if I had a second to chat.

I found a quiet space outside the cinema and they continued, "We wanted to put a call through to say that we loved your presentation. We thought we should let you know that we've decided to range your water and food products nationally." They added that they would consider the body care range, although they couldn't commit to it then and there, but wanted to let us know their decision on water and food straight away.

As our conversation wrapped up, they asked if they could announce their commitment that day.

I hesitated and asked if I could call them back. My head was spinning. "What the heck had just happened?" I asked myself.

This was not part of the plan. There was meant to be two or three weeks (or even months, some experts warned) of meetings, negotiations and waiting as they considered our proposal. They weren't meant to say yes after five hours!

I ran back in to the movie and was barely able to talk due to my state of disbelief, so I just told Justine we had to go. Hugh Jackman could wait for another day. As we walked to the car, I gave her the brief rundown: they had decided to take the range nationally – and they wanted to announce it immediately.

We had a quick phone call with Sarah and Jarryd, and all decided it would be best to try and stall them until Monday. That would give us time to think straight and figure out how to get some media on board to help announce it in a big way. Fortunately, the supermarket was happy to wait until Monday, so I pulled our team into my office to announce the exciting news and told them to keep it all under wraps until after the weekend.

OUR SECOND SUPERMARKET MEETING

On Monday morning, the supermarket announced their commitment to ranging our products in the media.

On Tuesday morning, right before our pitch with the second supermarket, I received a text message that read, "Check the *Financial Review*". This was a publication we'd never appeared in before.

I found a copy at one of the airport news outlets, flipped over the cover and right there on page two was a big photo and a headline that stated the first supermarket had said 'yes' "after a social pressure campaign". It couldn't get any clearer (and it couldn't have been more real) that the supermarket we'd met with first had got the jump on their 'arch rival', as the article so eloquently put it.

Due to this article and dozens of others like it, we were not too sure how this next meeting would go. With probably more nerves than we felt at the first meeting, but a little more confidence, we walked into the presentation room.

It was probably the hardest pitch of my life. The tension in the air was so thick that you could have cut it with a knife and in the first half hour or so, all my attempts at humour failed to generate a single smile in the room. After three-quarters of an hour, the atmosphere began to soften slightly as the team realised our intentions were to give both supermarkets the same opportunity, and that we had never intended for anyone to jump the gun. I think they too saw the potential of the fact that together, we could make a huge impact in the world.

Again I was reminded that we were sitting in a room with real people, not corporate robots. Yes, we'd made their life difficult, but once you cut through all of the hype, they were people just like the three of us.

On the way out, one of their executive team remarked, "You've turned the whole fast-moving consumer goods market on its head and every single major supplier has been talking about you." He said that in his 20-year career in grocery, he'd never seen anything like our campaign and from his personal perspective, he felt we should be proud.

As we walked to the car we were totally spent: emotionally, mentally and physically. At that moment, Justine and I had been unhappy with how the meeting went for a few different reasons. It took Jarryd to remind us that we'd actually done really well, especially when taking into account the result from the first supermarket and the success of the overall campaign.

Later that afternoon I had a few voicemail messages. One of them was from the second supermarket. They had decided to take the range nationally, including the body care products – a development that was mighty helpful in convincing the first supermarket to take the body range as well. That call came through three hours after our meeting.

Over two weeks, we had achieved something that even the biggest multinational brands in the world hadn't been able to do, despite the fact that they have access to millions of dollars in marketing. No one has ever had this many products, across this many categories, ranged within hours of the first meeting… Not to mention having almost no marketing budget and no track record in two of the three categories. It stumped everyone, including many industry experts and our own suppliers.

A veteran of the industry, who supplies many of our competitors, later said to our team: "You probably thought you created ripples when you launched that campaign. You didn't. You created waves. Every one of your competitors flipped out, because you challenged their empires." It's humbling to hear that because in essence, all we did was launch a YouTube video, fly a couple of donated signs below a helicopter and harness a bunch of public support. The campaign wasn't the challenge. It just lifted the lid on what we believe is one of the most powerful ideas behind Thankyou.

Why would you as a consumer continue to support a product that exists to build someone's empire or satisfy shareholders, when you could buy a product that exists 100 per cent to help someone else? Thankyou is a challenge to the empires and this campaign showed that consumers are ready to challenge the empires with us. Thankyou isn't a brand, it's a movement.

But back to the story. At this point we should have felt overjoyed, but the night after meeting with the second supermarket, we were feeling extremely flat and somewhat overwhelmed. Everything had gone to plan, except for the part where we would have a little time on our side. We had anticipated at least two or three weeks to recover from the campaign, after which we would hopefully get a commitment to stock the products in one or both of the supermarkets. From there, we would have been well placed to have products to market in the following months.

Instead, both supermarkets were pushing to get the products at exactly the same time: within one month. It was all happening so quickly. Once, we had thought that having three weeks to convert a bottled water concept into 50,000 bottles of water for one distributor was a challenge. We were now in for a real test, as this time we had four weeks to turn our tested product concepts into hundreds of thousands of units of product, and ship nearly $1 million worth of stock to 10 distribution centres.

I have a clear memory of sitting in a meeting with one of the supermarkets prior to launch. We were running through all the logistical details, which were quite complex. At one point, one of the eight people from their supply team in the meeting commented: "You had better make sure your entire supply and logistics team are right across all of this." Jarryd and I didn't quite have the heart to tell them that Jarryd, sitting at the table, was our entire supply and logistics team.

Here began the steepest learning curve of our lives.

SOME THOUGHTS TO TAKE AWAY:

ONE. Don't let 'expert opinions' dictate how you execute your idea. If we had created a 2-3 minute campaign video in line with expert advice, we would have struggled to communicate everything we needed to. There are times when you just have to trust your gut – even if it's risky.

TWO. No matter how prepared you are, there will always be times when things don't go to plan. The key is to prepare as well as you can, but at the same time train yourself to adapt to change and be solutions-focused in the moment.

THREE. There will always be people who don't believe in what you're doing. Most times, their opposition to your idea will only strengthen your resolve (as hard as their criticism can be to deal with at the time). I'll talk more about this later in the book.

FOUR. Remarkable ideas are contagious. The nature of our campaign inspired the supermarkets to break all the rules and say "yes" to our range in record time, and then roll the products out into stores in a timeframe that broke all industry standards.

FIVE. No matter how incredible you think your PR stunt is, no one will care about it if a royal baby is born on the same morning!

CHAPTER 1.9
Money Doesn't Change Everything

"If I just had enough money, then I could easily..."

Said anyone and everyone who has had an idea, ever.

When you're implementing an idea, it's tempting to think that if you could just meet someone rich and encourage them to give you lots of money, then you could make your idea a reality. There is no denying that at some point in your journey, many of you may require money.

But before you do, there is something much more valuable you'll need. Let me explain by sharing a story from Thankyou's past...

It was a warm Sydney night and I was with Morgan, one of our founding team members, at a conference. We had been on our feet all day, manning our stand, when one of the event organisers approached us with some exciting news.

He told us that he had scheduled 15 minutes into the diary of one of the major speakers at the conference for us to pick his brain. And as if that wasn't thrilling enough, we were told that this particular speaker was a self-made billionaire. We honestly couldn't contain our excitement. I quickly did the sums and worked out that if, by some miracle, this man chose to donate just 0.1 of a per cent of his money to our company, we would have $1 million in the bank.

We'd been waiting for what felt like years to meet someone like this. We knew that we had a solid business concept but one of our key challenges (or so we thought back then) was finding people who believed in our vision to back us financially… despite the (not-so-minor) roadblock that we didn't offer shares or equity in the company, as we are 100 per cent owned by our own charitable trust, which means we exist 100 per cent for impact.

In our heads, to change the world, all we needed was someone who was financially set to get behind us and give us some money. And on this particular summer evening, it seemed that our moment had finally arrived.

After battling a fair amount of pre-meeting nerves, Morgan and I managed to walk into the room somewhat confidently. We saw the man we were meeting, sitting at a large table in the corner of the room and as we approached, I couldn't help but mentally take note of a few things about him.

For starters, this man looked just how I imagined a billionaire would look. He was dressed in an immaculate suit with a pocket square, diamond cufflinks and a diamond and gold tie-clip. He had also taken his shoes off and placed them neatly together on the floor next to his chair, which I hoped was a sign that he was relaxed.

We sat down in silence and he simultaneously placed both hands in front of him on the table. He looked us both up and down and then, without smiling, said, "What do you want?"

Although I was caught a little off guard (there was no small talk, not even an introduction!) I jumped straight into my spiel. I tried to quickly explain who we were and what we did, which I hoped could lead into a conversation about the financial assistance we needed. About a minute into my explanation on what our organisation was all about, he cut me off and with a loud voice said, "Daniel, I asked you, what do you want?"

We were a little stunned. Morgan looked like he'd seen a ghost and I was trying to talk but words were just not coming out. Before I could squeeze out a sentence in response, he continued, "I get paid $25,000 for 15 minutes of my time by world leaders to advise them. I'm giving you this time, so tell me: what do you want?"

I somehow spluttered out that we were just two young guys who looked up to him, and that we wanted to learn what it took to achieve what he had. I then asked if he would be willing to work with us, to support us from a mentoring and financial perspective.

We won't forget his response in a hurry. In fact, I think his words are forever etched in our memories. "Stop wasting your time," he said bluntly. "Quit this rubbish and go and do something worthwhile with your lives."

He began telling us how his son, who he said had one of the highest IQs in the country, had completed a series of university degrees and was a roaring business success, before concluding that that's what we should aspire to. Then he asked, "Do you know what the richest country in the world is?" This was obviously not a question he wanted us to answer, since he answered it himself before we could even attempt a reply.

"Africa," he said (which, as it turns out, isn't even a country). "It's about time they helped themselves. I will never support something like this because it's a waste of time."

Once he had finished his speech he looked at me and said, "Is there anything else you want?" We were both frozen in our chairs, desperately hoping this was a bad dream instead of reality. I replied, "Well, we are so grateful that you have taken the time to meet with us. Again, it's inspiring for young guys like us to get to spend some time with you. I'm wondering if you have any final advice for Morgan and I?"

"Yes," he said. "Buy my book." The silence in the room was deafening. We stood up and walked quietly out of the room. Morgan and I didn't talk to each other as we slipped through the corridors, out of the venue and onto a pier in Sydney's Darling Harbour. It's hard to explain the feeling of having your high hopes not just dashed, but also literally lit on fire in front of your eyes. I felt like I'd just been punched in the face and I was choked up.

But right then, as we stood on the pier, we both started to laugh, and laugh pretty loudly. I remember jumping up and down while shaking my head at one point and repeating, "What was that? What was that?!"

Morgan and I spent a few more minutes laughing, shaking our heads, waving our hands and then we finished by hugging. Yes, hugging. It would be interesting to go back in time and ask the people looking at us what they thought was happening on that pier that day. It turns out we were learning a very valuable lesson; that money isn't always the answer to our prayers.

We thought that a big payday from our billionaire friend would give us the start we needed, but in hindsight, I'm glad we never got handed a golden cheque that warm summer evening. The thing is, with less financial restrictions comes the temptation to pump money into things simply because you've got the budget for it. In doing so, you run the very high risk of spending on something that's an average idea – and average ideas almost always bring average return.

An average idea with lots of money injected into it can achieve results – this happens all the time in advertising. Big companies with huge budgets pump out very average TV and billboard advertising campaigns all the time, and the results they accomplish are good enough for the people who signed off on them to keep their jobs. As Robert Stephens, founder of Geek Squad, says: "Advertising is the tax you pay for being unremarkable."

When you have no or little money, you are forced to focus on implementing the remarkable. This might sound like a stretch, if you're of the belief that remarkable ideas are expensive. But I've learned that truly remarkable ideas will always attract the money they require to work – all you need is a little momentum.

MOMENTUM CHANGES EVERYTHING

At one point in the early years of the Thankyou journey, I booked a 15-minute meeting with the Australian managing director of Wrigley, the world's largest chewing gum company. The intention of the meeting was to say a short thank you for a small partnership that we formed with one mutual retailer, and to quickly give him the rundown of what our organisation was all about. I walked into his office feeling pretty nervous because I wasn't sure what to expect.

Many people in important positions can be very direct (and even tell you to go and buy their book!) and when meeting with them, you can get the feeling that just by talking to them, you're wasting the oxygen in the air. This meeting ended up being the complete opposite of that scenario.

When I arrived, the MD shook my hand and then we walked over to the couches in his office and began to talk. Time flew by and 20 minutes in, I asked him if I should let him go. He proceeded to tell me he'd blocked out one hour for our time together. I was a little taken aback but he started sharing with me some of his lessons learned and most valuable insights. The meeting became less about the potential partnership and more about him helping to develop me.

There were many great insights shared in that one hour, but there is one that stands out; I've drawn on it many times since. "Momentum changes everything," he said. "Once you have it, keep it because it allows you to ask for things that you could never have asked for without it." This concept underpins all of our greatest moments and turning points in the Thankyou journey, and it's a concept that will change everything for you if you get onto it early enough.

You may have heard the expression "putting the cart before the horse". It's often used as a negative reference by suggesting someone is doing things the wrong way or in the wrong order. But I like the idea that by doing things the wrong way, you can sometimes have your cart pulling your horse. This is remarkable (people will literally remark about it). Why? Because no one notices horses that pull carts; they blend in. But people are intrigued by the cart that pulls the horse and might just want to get on board this phenomenon, which only adds to the momentum.

Back in 2011, we decided that launching a TV commercial would be a great way to take our brand awareness to the next level. We had heard from someone that television stations donate one per cent of their airtime to not-for-profits, so we figured it was worth a shot to try and obtain some free advertising.

We quickly figured out that, airtime aside, it can cost some serious money to produce a good-quality television commercial. We worked out that we had a few thousand dollars to invest into this project. This meant that no one was very keen to help us, because they were not too confident such a low-budget ad would even make it onto TV.

Unfortunately, we also learned that the one per cent of pro bono advertising space is highly sought after. We had further hurdles to overcome, like the fact that our organisation didn't quite fit the standard not-for-profit mould, even though we're a social enterprise that exists 100 per cent for impact.

It was interesting to discover how this game worked. Nearly every non-profit in the country pitches for the space, which was to be expected, but we were informed that some networks have longstanding partnerships with certain charities, making it harder for other organisations – ie us – to compete.

To give ourselves the best possible chance of being selected, we were advised to use our tiny budget to make the best-quality advertisement we possibly could, to present to the networks in the hope they would choose us over the hundreds of other submissions.

In this instance, we decided to well and truly put the cart before the horse, with the hope that this approach would get us a better result. We booked a meeting with a managing director at one of the major networks. Our pitch was fairly simple: we essentially walked in and shared our story and then said, "We'll produce one of the best Community Service Announcements (CSAs) you've ever seen. If you like it, play it. If you think it's no good, then we don't want you to play it." It wasn't your average pitch from someone trying to get free ad space. It's a known fact in business that you shouldn't over-promise something that you aren't 100 per cent sure you can deliver on, right? The thing is, we were naive enough to think we could deliver – and then some.

They seemed to love the Thankyou concept and the fact that we were so confident in our ability to deliver a high-quality production. Or perhaps they were fascinated enough to watch us attempt it? Either way, they replied that as long as the quality was as high as we promised, they'd air it. It was the closest we could possibly get to a pre-commitment and by using this strategy, we effectively edged out our competition and secured ad space.

Sure, there was one small stumbling block: we needed to make one of the best CSAs in the business, something that had seemed impossible just days earlier. Before this meeting, producers, editors and suppliers didn't want a bar of us, or our tiny production budget. But by getting the support of the network (and later on, other networks that came on board) we had created momentum. With this momentum, we were in a better position to ask for the other things we needed to help us make a world-class CSA.

Now, we just needed an idea.

CAPTURING THE 'THANKYOU WATER MOMENT'

Coming up with an idea that we could actually execute within our budget proved to be challenging, as anticipated. We'd tried to gain support from some leading marketing agencies, but it was evident that they were used to working with big budgets. They came up with plenty of ideas, but they had no way to execute them unless we were able to provide a bigger budget.

One night in our lounge room, Justine and I dreamed about the ad concept with another Daniel, a creative genius who would later work on our Coles and Woolworths Campaign. Together, we came up with the idea of capturing the 'Thankyou Water moment' in super slow motion – that is, the moment that takes place when a customer purchases a bottle and simultaneously becomes part of funding water projects.

The way Daniel described the concept visually sounded amazing and we were all excited. Daniel did flag that, in order to get an incredible result, it could only be filmed on a camera called the Phantom Flex, which filmed in super slow motion at 10,000 frames per second.

When we found out that this camera was worth $250,000 and would be very expensive to hire, at that moment I knew we'd hit the jackpot. Not because the camera had an awesome name (although that didn't hurt), but because this idea was so big and really so impossible that it might just work.

We started meeting production agencies and told them our idea, but we were quickly shut down when they found out it required the Phantom Flex and a shooting schedule of two days in Australia, followed by about five days in Cambodia. If that wasn't enough of an ask, we also needed to shoot water, which meant the camera would get wet – requiring a very expensive waterproof case.

It was explained to us that there were only two of these cameras in the country at the time, and they were usually hired out for around $12,000 a day for the camera alone. The waterproof case was in itself worth upwards of $100,000. We were told anything was possible if we had the budget for it, but clearly we didn't.

We weren't going to let the naysayers stop us, so we began to contact anyone we could find in the country who either owned or had a connection to someone who owned a Phantom Flex. One of our team got onto a guy named Andrew, who owned one of these magic cameras, and the good news was that he was open to meeting. I flew up to Sydney straight away to meet him.

After we sat down, I explained how we had this idea for a TV commercial and that we had the support of a major network to run it, provided the piece was of the highest quality. I invited him to use his talents to help make something remarkable and inspire Australians to join our movement. I told him we could cover flights to Cambodia plus food and accommodation for the duration of the short trip, but that we couldn't afford anything more. In other words, I was asking him to work for free, while using his very expensive equipment – and to commit seven days to our project with no financial return.

Andrew sat back with a pondering look on his face, then smiled and said he would do it. He later thanked me for giving him the opportunity to be part of the project, which I thought was crazy because we were so lucky to have him join us. As chance would have it, he had also filmed for Mick Fanning and other world pro surfers, so he had a waterproof case for the camera.

Andrew's commitment to our project that day was valued at well over $70,000. That's what we call momentum.

Following our positive meeting with Andrew, we wrote to one of Australia's best colourists (the term for people who colourgrade your ad), named Vincent. Because the networks were committed to air the advertisement and we now had both a camera and an operator – someone who was extremely respected in the industry – on board, he was willing to help out in a pro bono capacity as well.

Funnily enough, because the colourist had agreed to be involved, so too had one of the leading editing groups in Australia. They happened to be editing the new Coca-Cola commercial in the next room. We wrote to an international artist, Jonsi, who donated a song for the ad. All in all, by the time it went to air, over $110,000 worth of time and resources were donated to make our commercial happen.

Best of all, the networks loved the finished ad, which meant that as well as securing a heap of random late-night spots, our commercial also appeared many times in prime time, including during the cricket tests and the ARIA Awards. We discovered that the approximate value of one of those spots alone was worth $20,000! Over time, we ended up receiving hundreds of thousands of dollars worth of donated space.

How did we, a tiny little organisation (remember that this TV ad launched two years before the Coles and Woolworths Campaign), go from one of the thousands of cause organisations vying for free ad space, to one that actually secured the support of the networks?

It all came down to momentum. As we discovered, momentum truly changes everything.

DOES THIS CONCEPT ONLY WORK IF YOU'RE DOING SOMETHING CAUSE-RELATED?

You might be thinking that due to the nature of our company, momentum is easier for us to create than for others. Yes, our securing support from television networks did rely heavily on the fact that we exist purely for a cause. Having said this, the Wrigley CEO who shared his thoughts with me wasn't limiting the ability to create momentum to cause-driven organisations; after all, he ran a very corporate enterprise.

At the start of this book, I talked about the challenges we had in obtaining funding to get our idea off the ground. We had met with so many people and pitched them our ideas based on our cause, but stuff changed the day we began to gather momentum. By securing the bottling factory's commitment – which, when you look at it, was no more than "if you can sell it, we'll make it for you" – we were able to show Visy that we were serious.

Visy wouldn't have looked twice at us if we didn't have a factory lined up. And while they did donate 30,000 bottles to us because of our cause, they gave us the bottle shape for free mainly because it hadn't been used by any major brand and would still make them money from every bottle that we'd sell. While they gave us a leg up, it was still a good commercial deal for them.

Getting the factory and Visy behind us helped our pitch to MBC. They figured we had something going for us if we had these two big companies backing us, and they reasoned that if they didn't get in on the action, a competitor would.

Landing our first order for 50,000 bottles was the final momentum builder, which helped us raise the $20,000 we needed to register the company and cover all of the set-up costs involved.

I guarantee that if we walked around with a nice business plan asking people to donate or even invest $20,000 into a group – one with no experience and a big, bold, crazy idea that's up against global competitors who have literally saturated the market – we'd still be walking around today looking for funding. That was our first approach for months before we decided to find a way to create some momentum.

An example of the horse pulling the cart would be: find your $20,000 start-up capital, then register the business, and then try and get a distribution deal. But the cart pulling the horse scenario is: land the 50,000 bottle order, then figure out a way to find the $20,000 you need to register and set up the business.

As an organisation, we have used this key strategy in almost every way possible. We've had over 700 media features throughout our journey and nearly every major Australian television network, newspaper or radio station has covered our story. Media has been a huge part of helping create momentum, as lining up media commitments has helped us obtain more support from retail and corporate partners. You'd be surprised how lines like, "You may have seen us on *Sunrise* yesterday morning" or "We are in *BRW* magazine this week, and we were wondering if you'd be interested in…" help to open doors!

Our gala event in 2012 was a huge success and it's my belief that the greatest momentum creator there was David Koch, aka Kochie, the host of Channel 7's *Sunrise*. Him hosting the night was the first feature of the event that we locked in. We had barely any budget for the entire evening (as usual) and we'd never run a big event before, but the day I got the email from him to say he would fly down to host the event was the day that I knew the gala's success was a done deal.

Why? Because it made a big statement that this event was a serious deal and it gave us the momentum to get everyone else – from the caterers to the venue, to the print company, to the band – involved. We ran a world-class event because the reality is, everyone wants to be involved in an idea that's moving forwards and if they can get their seat at the table, they'll bring their best to it.

When you're trying to implement an idea, instead of getting stuck on the fact that you don't have the resources to make it happen, think about what it will take to create momentum to naturally attract others to get involved.

Originally, we had the vision to get our water into the mainstream, but we couldn't crack the retail market. We didn't have the budget or the other requirements to convince a retailer to get on board. So we created momentum with the 7-Eleven campaign, which presented an opportunity too good for them to say no to.

We replicated this strategy on a much grander scale when we pitched to Coles and Woolworths, and when rebranding as Thankyou in 2013. The development of the new product range needed serious funding, and then once we landed the supermarkets, we needed even more funding to manage the growth. Once we had momentum behind us from the campaign, the funding was a lot easier to obtain than before, when we were just running around saying, "We hope we'll get the supermarkets on board." Those campaigns were bold, innovative and a little bit cheeky, but ultimately they were constantly putting into practice one of the greatest lessons we've learned: momentum changes everything.

To make your ideas a reality you need momentum more than you need money. In time, everything else you need will come.

THE KEY TO BUILDING MOMENTUM? BE FAST

"It's not the big that eat the small, it's the fast that eat the slow." This quote, made by New Zealand tech entrepreneur Rod Drury, is a philosophy that we live by at Thankyou.

Why? It's because it sums up our fighting spirit. The reality is, each one of our competitors has hundreds or thousands of staff, with bigger marketing budgets and more resources than we could ever imagine. We'll never beat them in size, but we may just beat them with speed.

One of the most fundamental keys to disrupting the status quo is being fast. Fast to market, fast to innovate, fast to fail, fast to learn.

What is fast? Fast is Kirk, in our sales team, emailing our General Manager of Marketing, Sarah, late one afternoon with an idea inspired by something he'd seen on Facebook. I was copied in on the email and read it as I was walking into a meeting. I thought to myself, "I don't know if that's a good move; what if it doesn't work, we're too busy, it's the end of the day and we don't have the time for this, we don't want to be known as an antagoniser brand…"

However, by the time I was out of the meeting, Sarah had already made the decision to proceed and it was game on.

So, just what was 'it'?

It was April 2015, and Virgin Australia Airlines had just announced that they would now provide complimentary food to all passengers on board, in an effort to challenge the number one carrier in the country, Qantas. They then posed a question on their Facebook page on the day of the announcement, asking, "What food and drink products would you like to see on board?"

Kirk thought we should share it with our fans. Sarah agreed and after sharing Virgin's post, hundreds of people requested Thankyou products. The next morning, there were more than 800 comments on the post in support of Thankyou, which soon grew to 1200.

Then one of the team had an idea to tweet Sir Richard Branson. So we did: "Hey @richardbranson @VirginAustralia Overnight 800 responses to FB post in support of @thankyou_group. Thoughts??"

After that, we had a moment of realisation. Did we just tweet Richard? He's the king of this sort of publicity stunt, so what the heck were we doing? Our initial nerves dissipated once the tweet got retweeted to over 5 million people, before the media began covering the story, rehashing blow-by-blow accounts of our mini 'campaign'.

There is an online influencer in New York, who is ranked in the top one per cent on LinkedIn and top 0.5 per cent on Twitter, who joined in the conversation and shared our tweet with his 1 million-plus followers.

Then an influential BRW reporter jumped in, tweeting: "Veteran master of the publicity game @richardbranson faces challenge from Gen Y pretender @danielmflynn". I thought being called a "pretender" was a little offensive, so I responded with the tweet: "Just thought I'd ask the question off the back of fans going nuts for the Virgin post we shared. Pretender??" The reporter then replied with: "Pretender, as in 'to the throne'. Not a pejorative term. Look it up". I responded with,

"Ha. Got it! Should have finished uni!"

At this stage, we thought that since we'd taken this one to Richard and we were apparently challenging the throne, we had better step it up a level. Someone on our team knew a guy. She called him, and although he hadn't heard of our brand (a little disappointing), she explained what we needed and asked if we could count on his support. He said no. There was some back and forth over a number of phone calls and then at 12.37pm, he emailed us saying, "How soon can you get me artwork? If I have any window, it's right now!"

We had just a few minutes to whip together a design file and email it up to him. While this was happening, we called the news teams at Channel 7 and 9 and asked them to head to Virgin's head office in Brisbane. Twenty minutes later, a digital billboard truck arrived at the same destination, with a message that read: "Hey Richard! Love the question your team posted on Facebook... Looks like there's a truckload of support for Thankyou #ichoosethankyou"

Sure, "truckload of support" may not have been the best creative in the world, but it's all we could come up with in the short space of time we had to work with.

Within 24 hours, we reached millions of people through a campaign that didn't cost us a cent. The billboard driver donated his time, even though it was the first time he'd heard of Thankyou. My favourite comment I overhead that day was from one of our team, who said, "I went into a meeting hearing that we'd tweeted Richard Branson, and by the time I came out we had a billboard truck and media heading to Virgin's head office!"

Articles came out praising the speed to which we reacted. The former MD of Kellogg's Australia,

Jean-Yves Heude, was even quoted as saying that never in his 31 years of experience, had he ever seen a team turn around a communication campaign like this.

How do I know he made this comment? Because I was standing next to him! We'd got him on board to help coach some of our team and the day this campaign went down, he was in our office. At the end of the day he uttered in shock, "Never in my 31 years…" to which we all clapped. I called him later to thank him for his kind words and also to ask him if I could quote him in the media; we'd had a number of reporters call us and his statement would make an amazing quote.

This is an example of being fast. While it's this sort of thinking that will bring results, it's not easy. It involves trusting your team to make decisions. I wasn't 100 per cent on board when I saw the idea pop up in my email, but sometimes we have to trust others to fly with things and possibly fail and learn, or succeed!

After all was said and done, Virgin posted a response to us on their Facebook page, saying thanks for our little "drive by". We took this as a very positive sign!

So what happened next? We were fast and it was perfect, because it's Virgin and they are fast, right? Well, maybe we caught them on an off month. It was weeks before we were able to secure a meeting with the Virgin Australia team. While they're not handing out Thankyou muesli bars and bottled water on flights just yet, we're hopeful that a partnership between Virgin and Thankyou will eventuate in the near future! They seemed to be interested in being customer-led, especially if their Facebook post is any indication, so we're keeping optimistic. Watch this space!

Sir Richard Branson is a serious game changer; he always has been and always will be. When Virgin starts a business it is no doubt fast; we were experiencing an organisation possibly becoming slower as it got larger. Virgin Australia changed the game when they started with $10 million (most airlines start with ten times that), but today, it's a huge organisation with hundreds of moving parts and thousands of staff – no matter how awesome an idea is (even if it goes driving past on the side of a truck), it's going to take time to get it across the line.

Does this mean big organisations are slow? Does this mean that only the founders can truly live out game-changing type thinking and activity?

You might be tempted to answer yes. But then, let me remind you that the book in your hands was ranged by Shayne, Scott and Josh from LS Travel Retail within 24 hours of our first pitch meeting with them. They are not founders and their organisation has thousands of staff; they are one of the largest book retailers globally. Yet, they were able to think differently and change the game.

Were they fast? Yes. Did they take a risk? Yes. Was it uncomfortable? No doubt. Will it work? Maybe. We really hope so!

In other words, this isn't a concept for the one per cent. We can all apply this thinking. To change stuff you have to think fast and act fast, because that is what gives you the competitive edge. After all, it's not the big that eat the small; it's the fast that eat the slow.

SOME THOUGHTS TO TAKE AWAY:

ONE. Make sure your idea has the foundation of being remarkable, not just average. Average requires a lot of money to execute and will be forgotten tomorrow.

TWO. Don't fall into the trap of getting busy looking for money; the secret to success is to get busy creating momentum.

THREE. Once you have momentum, fight to keep it.

Fight for it with everything you can because it's one of the hardest things to create. When you have it you can ask for things that you never could have without it.

FOUR. Putting the cart before the horse is a great metaphor that's useful for all of us. Of course, it's not actually possible if you are literally in the horse and cart industry. Or is it?

FIVE. There are two definitions of the word 'pretender' and it's best not to mix them up… especially during Twitter exchanges with really smart guys.

CHAPTER 1.10
The Four-Letter Word: Fear

There is one four-letter word that, I believe, is capable of being the single greatest barrier holding each of us back from truly making our mark in this life.

Before I get back to the story and what happened once the supermarkets said yes, I need to talk about one word. You're likely to be familiar with it...

Fear.

You could be a CEO or a school student. You may have all the experience in the world or none at all. You may be part of a large, established, well-resourced organisation or work in a small start-up; been in the job 20 years or one week; about to step out onto the sports field or stage for the 50th time or the first time.

Regardless of person, prestige or position, fear can be present. But we must all overcome it in order to succeed, to make our ideas a reality. In some cases, we have to conquer it again and again.

The fear of failure has killed more dreams than failure itself, which is an interesting outcome. If you get the opportunity to talk to, listen to or read books from some of the most successful people in the world, they will likely tell you that their greatest life lessons were found in the ashes of their failure.

So if failure leads to learning, which then leads to success, you'd think that the concept of failure would be embraced in our culture, instead of rejected and feared. And yet instead, the fear of failure stops so many people from stepping out in the first place. Fear locks us up, silences our dreams and holds us back from ever taking the risks necessary to truly succeed.

There's no denying that failure hurts – it is lonely and painful and so it makes sense that the best way to avoid it is to not attempt anything that could fail. I know this from experience; during our start-up journey I led our team through our fair share of crushing failures.

The difference for us was that my naive and optimistic approach meant I wasn't too afraid to fail and learn from it. However, this mindset didn't just develop overnight. When I look back, I realise that it was cultivated from an early age, much earlier than when this story began at age 19. My mum talks about my passion for business as a child; apparently during my free time, I would attempt to close deals with my fellow kindergarten playmates for the latest batch of helicopters I had acquired. And by 'helicopters', I mean the seeds that fell from a tree in the kindergarten yard that looked like a helicopter blade.

I think the potential buyers may have had some reservations about buying them from me, when they could just pick them up off the ground themselves. This little venture failed. What's the lesson? I learned a thing or two about supply and demand and also a bit about the importance of selling a product that people might actually want to buy.

I guess you could call that my first experience as an entrepreneur – and as it turns out, it was the first of many.

DAYS OF THE OLD SCHOOLYARD

By the time I entered primary school, my entrepreneurial spirit was firing on all cylinders and I was making the most of whatever the latest craze was (my earliest lesson made an impression, and I refocused to ensure I was always selling something people wanted).

In the mid-1990s, when gobstoppers were in high demand, I was walking the schoolyard selling them from my fishing tackle box that I'd received for Christmas; it had never been used for fishing. It seemed like such a genius idea: all I did was purchase the gobstoppers in bulk from the supermarket; then sell them individually for between 5 and 10 cents each. After three months of pretty serious selling, I added up all the money I'd made and I couldn't believe the figures: I'd lost five cents. By lost, I mean I'd sold hundreds of these little gobstoppers, but my revenue less the costs of the gobstoppers (which I owed Mum, for the three months she had been bankrolling me) was minus five cents. I was so discouraged. I failed.

The lesson? I had eaten my profit. Quite literally. Business was booming, or so I thought, and I didn't see any issue with having a couple of gobstoppers myself here and there, and maybe even giving a few to my friends. I coincidentally had quite a lot of friends during that period of my life.

"Protect your profit", says every business book and lecturer. If you eat it (I'm sure they're talking metaphorically, not physically) by thinking you're doing well enough to withstand excessive spending, you will fail.

From day one at Thankyou we have protected our profits. We have a separate bank account (seasoned finance professionals may be having a laugh at this point) and from every invoice received we transfer our 'projected profit' into that account. Then every quarter we distribute profit to our projects overseas. It's unconventional but I know the perils of not protecting your profit and in our game, the stakes are a little higher than a gobstopper shortage. Our project partners bank on that profit coming through to continue their work in the field.

Back to my schoolyard ventures, when pet yabbies were the popular new obsession, I became a supplier in all things yabbies. A friend would catch them after school at the local lake and we'd sell them the next day from lunch boxes filled with water.

I hit a tiny roadblock after a few customers complained that the yabbies were no longer moving after they had purchased them. This was a serious quality control issue, but the more severe roadblock emerged when someone stole my yabbie net after it was left out overnight at the lake. Lesson learned: don't sell yabbies – it's cruel. I potentially also learned another thing or two about managing supply chains, without fully realising the significance of that lesson until later in life.

A stable income wasn't discovered until I made my way into the car washing business. It kept me busy from grades three through to six. The business was genuinely (nearly) successful; I made a good amount of money and most customers were happy with the work. There were always the haters who made comments like, "Why are there little scratch marks all over my car?" or, "Where is the Mercedes badge that is meant to be on my bonnet?" But I was an all-round positive young person, so these little issues weren't anything that I couldn't work through with them.

Eventually I employed two friends. I know what you're thinking – two employees, not bad at all for a school-aged child. I'll never forget the day my first two employees started working for me. Coincidentally, it was the same day that I lost my first two employees. There was something they didn't agree with about being paid $1 each to wash cars, while I earned $2 to stand back and supervise. Go figure?

Following that experience, I found it a little challenging to transition from a supervisor role back to washing cars. However, I learned a number of lessons; little gems on risk management, keeping the customer happy, the customer always being right and how not to treat staff. I wouldn't realise these lessons, or the significance of them, until many years later.

As I graduated to high school, the stakes got a little higher and so did the opportunities. The canteen (otherwise known as a dictating monopoly) sold cans of soft drink for $2, and I saw an obvious gap in the market for some competition. Before long I was making a healthy amount of money, selling soft drinks to fellow students for $1 a can. Needless to say, as my sales volume steadily increased, so too did my newfound unpopularity with the canteen lady.

This particular business venture was shut down by the principal, which was a little disappointing. But this was my stomping ground for discovering the 'wholesale' beverages game. I took a risk in buying the amount of stock I did. It was hard work keeping it cold so the product would better appeal to my customers, but it paid off (for a little while anyway).

What fascinated me the most was that people were willing to pay for convenience. In essence, there was nothing all that innovative about purchasing a 30-pack of cans from the local supermarket, keeping them chilled, and then selling them to my schoolmates for a healthy profit. By going direct to the supermarkets, my customers could have purchased these cans at half the price, but convenience meant that they chose to buy from me.

TRADING CURRENCY – AND MY EMOTIONS

As the years progressed, it became clear that selling products to classmates would only get me to a certain point. It was time to broaden my focus. In year 11, I started paper trading Forex currency and only a few months later, I invested all my hard-earned McDonald's income into it. Our school had introduced laptops, which was convenient because not only could I do schoolwork on mine, but I could also check how my latest trade was performing without being detected.

Trading Forex currency seemed like my greatest business idea yet. Not only was it a space full of big words and acronyms that made me feel really smart if I could pronounce them, but also, I was making returns of between 20 to 30 per cent per week! The banks were offering just a few per cent interest per year, so I was over the moon… Until I wasn't. One Friday evening just before midnight, I was sitting at the computer, waiting for a significant economic announcement that was about to be released. To my horror, the decision went the opposite way to what I had hoped and in three seconds flat, I watched that little line on my computer screen – the one that represented my money – swan dive straight down.

The program locks you out once you lose half your money, so it was all over. I was in shock. I managed to recover myself emotionally; I got back on my feet, thinking that the worst was behind me. I kept trading over the following weeks, only to lose half my money again about 10 days later.

I quickly decided to put that career path on hold. I learned more about myself in this little venture than I did about how currency works. For instance, I realised the importance of removing emotion from decision-making, an extremely hard thing to achieve when money is involved. When trading, my emotions went up and down with my profit.

The first night that I lost half my money, I was actually making money on a trade. As it got higher and higher I got so excited and that rush of adrenalin was so intoxicating, I wanted to make more money. So instead of getting out at my pre-determined point, I stayed in – and only minutes later lost everything. I had an exit strategy on paper, but my emotions and my pride got in the way. Through this experience I learned that I didn't have the discipline needed to succeed in Forex trading.

I never told anyone this at the time, but I also realised how judgemental I was becoming of other people. Because I was making a little bit of money (initially) on something that I knew wasn't easy to figure out, I started to think of myself as better, smarter and more accomplished than those around me. There's an old proverb that says, "pride comes before a fall". We are all people who have value, who have something to offer this world yet, there is an illusion that money, or a certain skill or ability, makes you somehow better than others. I had bought into this idea and I'm glad I fell back down to earth quickly.

By the time I reached year 12, technology was starting to get more traction and with Australia's high retail prices for the latest phones – the Nokia N91 was about to be 'the next big thing' at the time – I saw a great opportunity to buy and sell. I began importing them from Europe and reselling them through the local trading post for a significant margin.

After much searching, I settled on a legitimate wholesaler who was sourcing phones from the UK. I'm not sure if he realised that I was a school student; the fact that I could only call him between 12.30pm and 1.30pm or after 3.30pm didn't seem to register with him. I sent him money and traditionally, that's the point where you usually receive your phones. Unfortunately, I didn't.

He told me that "customs have rejected the package" and he apologised. The good news was that he was going to refund my money, until he broke the news that "it turns out customs have opened all the phone packaging, so they can't be resold, which means I won't be able to refund you." I'm still not ready to face reality 100 per cent on this, but I'm 99 per cent sure I was scammed. There were a few lessons here, but the biggest one for me was not to blindly trust people. I have a very trusting nature and it's hurt me a few times over the years. Trust is important, but so too is not just taking someone's word for it. Due diligence is key. I also should have just bought shares in Apple in 2006 instead of wasting my time trying to import Nokia phones.

By the time I reached 18, my failures certainly didn't equal success – they just equalled failure and a few quirky, valuable lessons. People I knew had a good little chuckle each time something didn't quite work out for me. Publicly, I laughed along too, but inside it hurt a little more than I outwardly let on.

I realise now that I was remarkably fortunate, because a series of consecutive failures meant I was able to build resilience against failure. At 19, when my perspective on business, money and the realities of millions of people being trapped in extreme poverty shifted dramatically, I had more than I realised backing me up. In a nutshell, I wasn't afraid to fail. Although I didn't realise it at the time, it was an incredible benefit.

Your stories, failures and lessons learned will be completely different to mine. What's important, though, is that you take some time to reflect on those times when things haven't worked out and ask the most basic (but most valuable) question you can: "What can I learn from this?" Some days the answer might be "not a lot". But you also may be surprised at just how much gold is already within you, if you take some time to clear the dirt and dig it out.

LETTING GO OF YOUR FEAR OF FAILURE

If the fear of failure has killed more dreams than failure itself, the next question you need to ask is this: Are you afraid to fail?

For organisations, I believe one of their biggest failures is creating a culture that doesn't allow people to fail and learn. If you're leading a team or organisation, you need to actively foster a culture that encourages creativity and game-changing thinking, rather than stifling it by not being willing to let people take risks that may potentially fail… but may also succeed.

The quintessential start-up culture is the opposite of how traditional organisations operate. It is inherently infectious, filled with risks, failure, big wins and some painful losses. The problem is that once a start-up's ideas become more established, the risks grow. Payroll and other financial commitments increase and as a result, management becomes less prepared to take the same risks that they might have in the early days. Over time, the pioneering culture that built the business or idea can vanish. How do we keep that? How do we go back to that? By letting go of our fear of failure.

There was a part of me that didn't want to share all these stories of my failures with you, because they don't paint me in a particularly favourable light. One or two quirky anecdotes might be funny, but there are a few too many failures shared for my comfort.

Another part of me recognises that if you're going to make your ideas a reality, you can't afford to live in fear of what other people think. So I shared my entrepreneurial stories from my early days, warts and all; I hope they gave you a few chuckles!

I didn't always have this attitude towards other people's opinions. In fact, it wasn't long ago that I was ruled by what others thought of me. In year 11, for instance, I was convinced that I would never be able to do public speaking. That's because when I was in high school, from year nine onwards, I developed a strong lisp. I'd like to take this moment to point out that I'm a little frustrated with whoever came up with that word to describe the condition; even telling people you have a lisp is humiliating.

As a teenager, it felt like a crippling setback. When I talked, I would consciously try to choose words that didn't contain an 'S' sound. You can imagine how frustrated I was when I fell in love with a girl named Justine. I would call her "J" to avoid having to pronounce the 's' in her name, and she would point out, "Nobody calls me that!"

I told myself that I would never, ever, do public speaking because I was wrapped up in my fear of what I sounded like to others. What if I messed up my words; what if I stumbled? What would people think of me?

Every person battles fear in one way or another and the truth is, fear attempts to squash the greatness within every one of us. For me, it was a speech impediment. I spent hours with speech pathologists, thanks to my parents, who over time helped rid me of it. You'd think my fear of public speaking would have disappeared with my lisp, but funnily enough, it didn't. Even after the lisp was long conquered, any time I was asked to speak in front of a group I would get incredibly nervous and physically felt locked up inside.

This is the part of the story that still gives me goosebumps.

Since we launched Thankyou in 2008, I've spoken to millions of people through hundreds of interviews, including most of the major television and radio networks. I've been invited to speak at schools and universities and I now get invited to speak in front of thousands of people – including CEOs, directors and employees of some of the ASX 100 and Fortune 500 companies – as a professional corporate speaker.

I find myself on speaking lineups at conferences in Australia and around the world with incredibly prominent executives and entrepreneurs who have started million, even billion-dollar companies, not to mention the Olympians, famous musicians, sportspeople, comedians and media personalities. It's been an incredible opportunity that has helped spread the Thankyou story far and wide.

As I sit in the speaker's lounge before these events or backstage talking to high-profile people, I still have to pinch myself and I often find myself wondering, "How the heck did I get here? Should I tell someone I don't actually have it all together like these other people do?" But then, maybe no one has it as 'together' as you think they do.

What happened to that fear that used to stop me speaking in front of even a small group of people, let alone share the platform with famous people in front of a crowd of thousands?

THREE QUESTIONS THAT WILL MOVE YOU FORWARDS

One of my life mentors, Russell, once posed three questions to me that shook me to my core; he mentioned he'd read them in a book. I often ask myself these questions in those moments when I'm standing behind the curtain, preparing to step out on a stage, just before a media interview, or especially as I walk into a meeting to deliver a big pitch.

Just as I have asked myself hundreds of times now, I encourage you to ask yourself these questions:

- How would you live your life if you had no fear?
- What would you say?
- And what would you do?

Now pause, close your eyes, imagine. Don't rush over it, just consider your answers. Because after a moment or two, you and I get a glimpse of what our lives could be like without fear. What that speech could look like; what that presentation could achieve; what that new job or new career could bring. What that dream we finally decide to chase could result in, and what life-changing decisions we would make.

At that moment of asking those three questions, you have just a split second to make a choice that only you can make. You can choose to live that moment out, or you can choose to shrink back into that cage of fear that has tried to hold you back from doing remarkable things with your life.

For me, even writing this book meant that I had to overcome substantial fears and insecurities. Why? Simply because it has the potential to fail. Traditionally, you're not meant to write a book when you're at our early stage of the journey. I feel that perhaps I should have waited until Thankyou was an even bigger success story – a legitimate household name, or maybe when we had more products or had conquered international markets.

You're meant to wait until you and your team have well and truly made it before you write a book, aren't you? Then, as you near or farewell middle age, you write a book to reflect on your decades of successful years in business.

I made a different decision, to write a book like no other book has ever been written before, and the team backed the idea. We thought we'd write it as we progress on our journey, chapter by chapter (book by book). And we thought we'd invite you to write the future with us and walk this journey alongside us, simply by buying this book and investing into Thankyou's future.

Our dream is that there will be many more chapters (books) to come and that one day, when we are at that point where our dream has become a full-blown reality, people will say that they got to do something truly remarkable by walking our journey with us. That they got to grow as we grew, dream as we dreamed and ultimately, we hope that it's not just our story that will prosper – but also the story of thousands of people who read these chapters, learn from our lessons and go on to see their own dreams become a reality.

We think people need to see the real journey as it unfolds, not just read the highlights 30 years from now.

But hang on a second. What if we fail? What if this book only sells a couple of hundred copies? What if I'm a terrible writer and people don't like it? What if there are no more chapters because our organisation gets overtaken by competitors or the failing economy? What if the haters come out in droves and don't just attack the book, but me personally? What if we don't ever go on to actually see our dreams become a reality? What if the years behind us have been the best we'll ever have?

Well, then even that would make an interesting *Chapter Two*, wouldn't it – remembering that although failure can be painful, it is also a master mentor.

These are the questions and thoughts and concerns that swirl around my head, even now as I write this very page. I have a choice, and if you're reading this book right now, it means that I decided to ask myself what I would do if I had no fear. Then just for a moment, I pictured what that looked like... And, I made a choice to live that out and keep writing.

The truly remarkable thing I have learned is that if you're willing to let go of your fears, the most incredible opportunities have a way of presenting themselves. Earlier, we talked about how the fear of failure has killed more dreams and ideas to the grave because of fear that you may fail. What if our world needs your dream?

Overcoming fear is a personal battle we all face and I firmly believe that you cannot turn your ideas into reality until you break through this barrier. Note that overcoming fear isn't about completely blocking everyone out. I still consider the opinions of those closest to me, and others who influence my life, and I welcome their constructive feedback – but I don't *fear* what they think and I don't let them dictate my next move.

This book is as much about your story as it is about my story and our team's story, so let me ask you these few questions one more time.

How would you live your life if you had no fear?

What would you say?

And what would you do?

SOME THOUGHTS TO TAKE AWAY:

ONE. Sometimes the little stories of our life that we think are embarrassing can hold the most value. What are yours?

TWO. Living for the approval of others and to avoid criticism will lead to a loss of focus and a lacklustre approach. Create a culture in your life and in your team that allows people to fail and learn from it. Store these three questions in your memory for future reference. If you ever see me before I make a presentation or a big announcement about Thankyou, it's probably the answers to these three questions that I'm running through in my head! As a refresher, they are:

– How would you live your life if you had no fear?

– What would you say?

– And what would you do?

THREE. If you want to find a way through fear, don't attempt to go it alone. You've got to build that team around you to support you. Fear isolates; don't let it.

FOUR. I've heard it said that you should embrace fear, as it lets you know you're on the right track. I agree that fear can steer you in the right direction, but I don't agree that you need to embrace it. Fear is inward-focused – it becomes all about you and how you feel, rather than what you are about to do. Reject it.

CHAPTER 1.11

Partnering With Dreamers, Believers And Haters

Throughout our relatively short start-up journey, I've encountered many different people who have had an impact on our business.

I've come to realise that there are essentially three groups of people in this world who will take up most of your time and headspace, as you build your dream and attempt to make your ideas a reality. These three groups are the dreamers, the believers and the haters. I guarantee that at some point throughout your journey you'll have representatives from all three surrounding you.

As a leader, it's about finding the perfect balance between these three groups by paying enough attention to each piece of the puzzle, without letting yourself get influenced too fiercely in any one direction. If one group becomes too loud, you're in trouble. You could start to believe your own hype or begin doubting everything you do. Either way, the results can be crippling.

Take Facebook, for example. The dreamers are the team behind Facebook who dream day in, day out as they create and refine a platform that over 1 billion people use around the world.

Then there are the believers – they're the people like you and me, who 'believe' in the Facebook vision to some degree, or at least enough to actually sign up to Facebook and interact with it far too many times each day.

Lastly, there are the haters. These guys are the ones who are convinced Mark Zuckerberg is part of the CIA and that Facebook is some sort of government conspiracy. You can sit down with these people and try and reason with them or post really long, reasoned responses to their online rants, but they know what they want to believe and you're unlikely to change their minds.

This summarises the dreamers, believers and haters – and from my experience, each of these groups plays its role, existing together in some sort of dysfunctional harmony.

The dreamers

These are the people who are crazy enough to believe that your idea just might work, and they're willing to volunteer their time, skills or passion to help you build the dream. Even paid staff are volunteers to some extent, as they could work for anyone, yet they voluntarily chose to work for you. Sometimes in this team of dreamers, you'll have some pretty interesting debates, arguments and disagreements, all of which are very healthy when it comes to refining your dream and making it a reality.

The believers

Like the dreamers, this group is also crazy enough to believe in the dream and while they may not be in a position to work with you to build it day in, day out, they will do whatever is possible within their power to support you. The believers are *crucial* to your success. In an extreme case, to use Apple as an example, these are the people who line up throughout the night to be the first to glimpse the new iPhone or iPad. In a less extreme example, this is your target audience, your customers and your loyal supporters. It's so important that you're able to listen to their thoughts and feedback because without them, you're nothing.

The haters

Haters gonna hate. Some hate because they feel they have a legitimate reason, others just do it because it's what they do. You can aggravate them because of the way you styled your hair that morning, or because they fundamentally oppose what you aim to achieve. They will not only fail to participate in building your dream or idea, but they will actively vocalise their negative viewpoint.

CAN'T WE EXIST WITHOUT THE HATERS?

Undoubtedly, you're going to love the first two groups. For us, it's a huge honour to have people who love and support our vision. Every day we receive new product ideas and suggestions from our passionate supporters through social media, email, events, and even at dinner table discussions, and we absolutely love hearing them. That said, we also appreciate the contribution of the haters. You might be expecting me to rip into this group, but I'm not going to. I've heard it said that criticism is the mark of success and I have to agree.

Of course, that's a perfectly nice saying in theory, but when you're in the middle of fielding criticism, it can be a bitter pill to swallow. It can also make you question whether you are actually succeeding or epically failing. But I've learned that you need the haters and you need the critics, for two reasons.

The first reason? They keep you humble, which is so important. The moment you think that you're all that, you're stuffed, so when the critics criticise, it brings you straight back down the earth. (I'm speaking of legitimate critics who have potentially legitimate points to consider, not just ignorant people claiming you are an idiot for no reason!)

The second and equally important need for haters and critics is that they refine you and your dream.

You don't want to be surrounded only by dreamers and believers, whose feedback is so positive you mistake it for a compliment, because sometimes those two groups of people are too close to what you do to really call you out.

'Haters' is a pretty strong word and it may not best describe this group of people, because some of your haters don't really hate you (hopefully) – they just don't understand you or can't see your vision. This is why they'll question you or challenge what you're doing. It's very easy to let these little comments or pieces of feedback bring you down, but occasionally, this group may actually have a point.

You've got to be willing to explore every angle and even if you know they are wrong, it's that process of looking at what you do that refines you and makes you stronger. We learned this lesson first-hand after finishing our Coles and Woolworths Campaign. The media attention continued and the requests for interviews and time with various journalists and reporters were consistent. However, there was one particular interview that was different to the rest.

When the reporter called, it was clear she wasn't going for a positive news angle. I agreed to her interview, and I made the decision not to take a PR person with me. When I sat down with her and another reporter who was helping write the story, I opened by saying, "I live by this crazy idea that if there's nothing to hide then there's nothing to hide, so ask away."

What was meant to be a short interview turned into a two-hour drilling session. These two reporters went pretty hard. I don't mind answering robust questions, but there seemed to be a clear agenda behind their line of questioning. It was as if they had made their minds up that they were going to find something wrong with us, and they were determined to uncover some dodgy dealings. They explained that they'd been following us for about a year and they showed me printouts containing quotes I'd made in the past – sometimes years earlier – along with a whole stack of other personal information. Each time they proposed some sort of question while looking for the 'deeper hidden meaning', I was able to provide logical answers that cleared the air.

Eventually, it emerged that the main reporter was convinced that something scandalous was going on because I'm a Christian and I go to church, and two of our four project partners at the time had a faith base.

We work with many global non-government organisations, some who have a religious affiliation and some who do not. Keep in mind that 20 of the 25 largest aid charities in Australia (and many globally) have a religious affiliation, but their religious work must always be separate from their development work, or they automatically lose their charitable status. Australian law and our agreements with each partner do not let them use funds allocated for development work for religious purposes.

Towards the end of our interview, I could see the frustration on her face. She had hit me with every question and probably didn't expect me to have an appropriate answer to each and every one. She then asked a question that was so fascinating, it still stands out to this day: "How is it that your start-up has had more media support and more 'in-kind' support than any other start-up I've ever heard of?"; I felt a tone of accusation in her voice.

She turned to the other reporter for confirmation, who nodded, apparently in agreement that we had somehow engineered unfair special treatment. It felt like they thought there *had* to be some kind of secret agenda behind what we do at Thankyou, because to them it just was not possible that we genuinely wanted to help people, and that the public had genuinely gotten behind our cause.

My answer was pretty simple. "We are an organisation that exists for the sole purpose of helping others, so I think people want to get behind us because they have the opportunity to be part of something bigger than themselves," I said.

She still looked frustrated. The interview ended shortly thereafter.

HOW TO RUIN A PERFECTLY NICE SUNDAY MORNING

A week or so later on a Sunday morning – my one day off – our exhausted team were recovering from a hugely successful, yet massive campaign. I woke up to a barrage of text messages from friends and colleagues within Australia and around the world, saying things like, "Don't worry, it will pass". There were dozens of similar messages filled with nice, encouraging words that seemed incredibly lovely but also very concerning. I felt a nervous pit begin to form in my stomach; I figured this was going to be an interesting day.

I mustered up the courage to find out what had prompted this friendly outpouring of support. The two reporters I had met with earlier had published a sensationalised article, which attempted to destroy our organisation's integrity by calling into question how our funds were used by one of our NGO project partners. It had a sensational heading and first paragraph (the part that everyone reads) but then fizzled out into nothing – which was probably because there was no real story behind it. The article caused a bit of a stir. A number of our corporate partners freaked out momentarily and we received a barrage of attention on social media following its publication.

The release of the article attracted a whole bunch of haters and trolls, who spent the next week trying to discredit us as much as possible. There was, understandably, some genuine concern from loyal supporters as a result of all this activity.

Once we sent out a response to our partners and supporters that stated our position, including the actual facts, the whole thing blew over very quickly. As some would say, it was a storm in a teacup. The reality is that if our partners, or we, were doing anything wrong, it would have pulled us down completely.

After hundreds of positive media features, we suddenly had two reporters attempt to discredit our entire organisation and I took it to be a pretty personal attack. I am a 'words' person. This means that if someone verbalises something positive about me or what I'm doing, I feel really encouraged. I'd go so far as to say that it's often the words in a card that make me feel more valued than the present itself (except I still like presents… just saying).

On the flip side, when someone writes a scathing article attacking my dream, my integrity and what I have worked so hard to establish and build, I take it pretty hard. Even though I knew these reporters didn't have anything to firmly base their accusations on, the feeling of being personally attacked in such a hateful way was not a pleasant experience.

After reading the article, I wrote a response to our supporters, which we posted online (you can read it for yourself by Googling 'Thankyou Dan's response'). It clearly outlined each point made in the article and our actual position. I finished the response with one of my favourite quotes by Mother Teresa: "If you're kind, people may accuse you of selfish, ulterior motives. Be kind anyway."

On reflection, it was probably a little cheeky to end my response to an article that attacked us for working with a religious aid organisation, by quoting one of the world's most famous religious figures! At the end of the day, I actually think this negative article – regardless of how upsetting the experience was – helped strengthen the movement backing Thankyou.

After the article came out, thousands of people went into bat for Thankyou because they knew the truth. I've had many conversations with people that start with, "I heard about you because of that article", and while I smile at how negative news travels better than positive news, I recognise that because of that single media clipping, I've had the chance to share the facts with many pessimists, which has turned them into supporters.

Furthermore, the whole experience showed us that we live in a world where people are sceptical of others who are setting out to help and give back, which meant that we needed to address every possible concern.

As a result of this article, we reviewed our partnership policies to ensure that every aspect of every project we funded would live up to even the most intense public scrutiny. After all, we aim for there to be no blockages for people to buy Thankyou products, as our goal is to get as many people purchasing as possible.

Our experiences with haters have brought about some of our biggest insights, and our organisation is all the better for it. You'll likely have similar experiences and although they're no fun to live through at the time, they ultimately strengthen your organisation and open you up to looking at things from a completely new perspective.

SOME THOUGHTS TO TAKE AWAY:

ONE. In any form of leadership, particularly during the process of taking your ideas and making them reality, you'll encounter all three groups: the haters, believers and dreamers.

TWO. I used to feel incredibly uncomfortable at the thought of upsetting anyone. I've had to grow up and realise that in my role as a leader and to be successful, I am at times going to upset people in all three groups. I can't take it personally.

THREE. The challenge is to learn to take what you need from each group, without letting anyone – no matter how good or bad their intentions are – pull you away from your vision. Your very success may just depend on it.

FOUR. Positive and negative feedback has a way of throwing you into an emotional high or low. Both of these extremes have the potential to be dangerous and you have to find a way for your emotions to stay as balanced as possible on your journey.

FIVE. I value feedback and genuine concern, but deeply dislike a culture that encourages us to hate on something because we don't understand it. At Thankyou, we have a quote on the wall that says, "We rise by lifting others." Can you imagine a world that lived by this philosophy?

CHAPTER 1.12
Playing Hide-And-Seek In The Dark

We were only days away from our products hitting shelves.

Jarryd hung up the phone. He'd just finished an all-important conversation with a major supermarket, confirming orders for delivery. I turned to him with a massive grin on my face and said, "Do you think the person on the other end of the phone pictured you here doing this when they were speaking to you?"

We all had a good laugh; at that moment, Jarryd and I were standing on a golf course with the other guys from Thankyou. We probably should have been in our office working around the clock; no doubt that's what the other person on the phone would have expected.

But here's the thing. Our grand plan didn't quite go to plan. The marketing campaign had been a huge success and our meetings with supermarkets went extraordinarily well, all as planned. However, the fact that they took our products within hours and then wanted product *within weeks* was definitely not planned!

We were anticipating that we would have a week or two, if not a month or longer, of going back and forth with Coles and Woolworths before they eventually agreed to range our products.

During that time, we anticipated that our team would have time to recover. Prior to the campaign we were all on the edge of burnout and launching the campaign carried the risk of taking that burnout to the next level.

But we were so high on adrenaline, we didn't realise the crash that was about to come. After the supermarkets took our products, we spent a few days working extremely hard to meet their demands, and then realised that unless we did something drastic, we were all going to collapse. So what did we do? We booked a house near the beach and told all our staff to pack their bags for a two-day retreat. At this retreat, we weren't going to do any annoying team-building exercises or discuss anything even remotely work-related. Instead, we were just going to rest, hang out and celebrate our big win.

The chairman of the largest investment bank in Australia once gave me a few minutes of his time. After I explained what we did, he asked me a question I'll never forget. He said, "Do you celebrate the wins?"

"Yes, of course," I automatically replied. He said "When? What day and how did you celebrate?" Awkward pause. I couldn't answer. Why? Well, we actually didn't celebrate the wins. We didn't 'enjoy' success. I remember when we landed 7-Eleven Australia and I said to the team that it was a great moment, but we've really got our work cut out for us as we go up against the biggest brands.

Once we outsold one major brand, there were more to get, then more retailers and more products. I know what you're probably thinking: "I would hate working with you." You probably would have, back then. I didn't understand the importance of celebrating a win. Enjoying success felt wrong, because there was always more to do.

I've now come to realise there will *always* be more to do. Before you go again, you must enjoy the win.

With the Coles and Woolworths Campaign being our biggest win to date, the plan was to celebrate together on our retreat, to reflect on the journey, but also to rest. This retreat was unlike any work retreat I'd personally ever been on; I may or may not remember playing hide-and-seek in the dark at about 2am.

From a purely rational perspective, as an organisation that was preparing to launch multiple products into three new categories in the highly competitive fast-moving consumer goods market, challenging multiple global giants – perhaps we *shouldn't* have been in a beach house, playing hide-and-seek in the dark just weeks out from our launch. Maybe, maybe not. It was fun regardless, and it was exactly what each of our team members needed… to switch off and relax.

The point of this story? Sometimes, we can all let the seriousness of our mission and the job in front of us steal from the child within us. It's the little child inside of you that believes nothing is impossible. It's that child inside of you that dares to dream, dares to break the boundaries and is naive enough to believe that you might actually see your dream become a reality.

I'm not suggesting that playing hide-and-seek in the dark is necessary to your success (although it was great fun, you should try it!). But I am saying that you have to make sure you remember to celebrate throughout the journey, to enjoy the process and let out your inner child.

Interestingly, that spontaneous game of hide-and-seek in the dark was a great metaphor for where we were as an organisation. We knew what our objectives were, but this was completely new territory and in some respects, we felt like we were walking around in the dark, occasionally bumping into things (getting quite a few scares) as we navigated the path towards our goals. Straight after the retreat ended, we hit the ground running. With the team feeling refreshed, we were bouncing from meeting to meeting and getting ready for the official product launch.

We found it really bizarre that both supermarkets were almost fighting to get the product delivered before the other. It didn't stop there; we met with other independent supermarkets that were all keen to be part of the launch and they wanted it before Coles and Woolworths. We even had requests like, "Can we get our delivery even just one hour before they get theirs?"

It was crazy! For years, we'd struggled to get national support in any supermarket and now here we were, with all the major players in the market fighting to get our entire product range – most of which had no track record in the market – before the other. You'd think we were set to become one of the most successful start-up stories in Australian supermarket history. The truth is that we were far from that.

A DAVID AND GOLIATH BATTLE

It frustrates me when people underestimate us – and I have to say, it happens a lot. Many have predicted that we'll be a 'fly by night' story, in one day and out the next. Some prominent industry experts have mentioned that we don't have what it takes to make it; they think we'll eventually get squashed by our competitors or the hardball tactics of the supermarkets.

On certain days, after certain setbacks, I have wondered if they may be right. We were told that to survive in the supermarket space, we'd have to pay a merchandising company a large percentage to make sure our product is stacked properly on the shelf. The grocery industry is like a war

CHAPTER ONE

for suppliers, we discovered, and competitors will often move products around and play other games to influence sales. We were therefore told that we needed to partner with a merchandising company or we wouldn't last.

As a result, we had already spent months lining up a market-leading merchandising company to be our frontline representatives. Everything was locked and loaded and they were excited. Then suddenly, they flipped; after the campaign was successfully executed and the official launch was impending, I received an all-too-familiar call: our merchandising company was dropping us. I couldn't believe it. We didn't have time to get a new company on board before launch.

It turned out that it was purely a political decision on their behalf. One of our competitors in the muesli, oats and muesli bar categories had just signed a deal with this merchandising company and had told them that if they didn't drop us, the deal was off the table. This competitor was a $50 million business and we were worth nowhere near that amount!

During the call, our contact regretfully informed us that it was a "commercial decision". I told him, "You better believe it's a commercial decision. To walk away from Thankyou could one day be the biggest mistake you've ever made." The decision wasn't his to make but he did say that on a personal note, he hoped we would blow it out of the water. I'm sure the pun was intended – they usually are!

By a strange twist of fate, a few days later we received a call from another merchandising company that had just lost their contract with a $50 million dollar business! Their representative came in and presented the story of how he and his team had built this other company from almost nothing to a

$50 million dollar business. It was a big call to make, but it did look impressive on the graph in his slide presentation.

They wanted some pretty high rates for their services and we went back and forth many times over prices. The problem for us was that we needed to fund our projects from our profits, and the margin they wanted ate heavily into that. We pushed and pulled and finally we were close to an agreement. Then, literally days out from our launch into supermarkets, they contacted us to say that they were not comfortable moving forward with us. I remember the phone call so clearly. In fact, when I got off the call I tweeted, "If I ever write a book, the guy I just got off the phone with will get his own special mention."

At the time, I was so angry that I figured I'd publish this guy's name for sure. But I have since calmed down and realised that he probably wasn't the only decision maker and that he was just doing his job. Later, he even introduced us to another company – so while we launched without any merchandising support initially, a few weeks in we found a group to help us out.

However, during that phone call he said that they would be pulling out from partnering because their board didn't think we had what it took to be successful in grocery. He'd been talking to people internally in the supermarkets and they had also said that we had no "friends" inside, and we wouldn't be able to recover from the damage that our "ambush" campaign created.

As if that wasn't bad enough, his next words were, "You're not going to last." Trying somewhat unsuccessfully not to raise my voice I replied, "You do realise that you're not the first person in our five-year history to say something like this?"

People have *always* told us what we can't do and what we won't be able to do and we prove them wrong every time. Comments like this only motivate us further. This wouldn't be the last time someone would remind us of just how small we were and how unlikely we were to win this David and Goliath battle.

OUR SUPERSTAR PRODUCT, WHICH ALMOST NEVER LAUNCHED

Product did hit the shelves, albeit with a few hiccups, and I'm pleased to say that we shocked some people. The biggest surprise was our body care range. Initially, both supermarkets said that the hand wash product was their biggest concern. One of them wasn't even prepared to take it because they had all the data and research to prove that a premium product wouldn't sell in the supermarket.

We had developed a premium product that could compete with other bottles sold for $20 to $30 in pharmacies and boutique stores. But we weren't stocking our product with those retailers; instead, while retaining that high level of quality, we were launching into supermarkets at an 'everyday' price of around $8.

It seems cheap when compared to other premium products already stocked in supermarkets, it was the most expensive hand wash price on the shelf. We were told they had data to back up the fact that they believed this product wouldn't work. For that reason, both supermarkets were almost not even willing to give it a go. However, our research showed us that this product was going to fly. Our market study was more of the 'feedback from internal team and close friends and family' type of study, so it was possibly on a different scale to the research they had, but we believed in our positive gut feeling.

Thankfully, they both gave us a chance. We were given a hurdle rate that we had to hit within about six months or we would lose our space on the shelf. Within the first few months, we doubled and then tripled that rate! Since that point, we've continued to outsell every global competitor with some of the best customer loyalty rates you can get. It's been a huge success.

As a consequence, both supermarkets have taken on more of our body products. We now have over 12 products on the market in our body care range alone! I remember reading an article in *BRW* talking about how it all kicked off when we "cracked the supermarkets with the most expensive hand wash on shelf". The irony wasn't lost on me that this product nearly didn't make it to market at all. Weeks before launching the Coles and Woolworths Campaign, we had some big issues with the fragrance and it looked like all of our hard work had come crashing down.

Jarryd and I were both pretty much ready to pull the pin on this category of products; we figured we could look at re-launching it later down the track. But this range was Justine's 'baby' and she wasn't going to let it go down without a fight. We were having emergency meetings in our office with suppliers and experts during the two-week campaign. That's right – *during* the campaign. When sitting in these meetings, I often doubted that it was ever going to work. At Thankyou one of our core values is 'solutions-focused', and so through the creative solutions of our team (and with the support of experts in the field and an international leader in fragrance development) we pulled it all together.

The feedback from the public on both the muesli bars and muesli and clusters was (and still is) remarkable – people love the taste and quality. Callum, our Chief Taste Officer, our product team and suppliers have done an incredible job with these products. The only challenge for us is that this particular market is known to be one of the most competitive on the shelf. We are certainly feeling that pressure, but we're up to the challenge!

I mentioned earlier in this book that the former managing director of Kellogg's had described Thankyou as "the Apple of the fast-moving consumer goods industry". It's humbling to know that people of his standing are taking notice and are encouraging of what we're doing.

Right after this happened, I had a string of extraordinary encounters that have combined to give me an underlying confidence that we are heading in the right direction. I was being introduced by an emcee at an event and got an unexpected confidence boost I never saw coming when he shared a story with the audience. You see, the emcee had been at a different event where the outgoing CEO of Coca-Cola Amatil Australia was on the panel. During the Q&A section, a young guy asked what advice he would give to someone starting a beverage business in Australia.

The CEO said something cheeky like, "Don't bother, we've got the market covered." While his lacklustre response deflated the room, our emcee (as an audience member at that particular event) put up his hand and asked, "What about Thankyou Water?" The outgoing CEO apparently paused. "Well," he shrugged. "There you go."

You might think that it was simply a small, inconsequential comment. But you don't know how many times we were told, "Don't bother, they've got the market covered", by people who knew the market inside out. We could have taken that advice and never started. But we didn't – we set out on what seemed like an impossible mission and now the one reason that we should have never begun (a multinational company, no less) had started to take notice.

Our team received some industry data that our water was ranked as the number three water in the entire convenience industry. Above us were 250ml Red Bull and 600ml Coca-Cola – not bad to be sitting up with the biggest beverages in the world.

Then there was the time that I was invited to speak to the leadership team at Unilever Australia and New Zealand. Unilever are one of the biggest multinationals in the world; they own brands like Lipton, Streets, Dove, Lynx, Omo and dozens more. Globally, their products are apparently used 2 billion times a day in over half of the households on the planet. Their Australian and New Zealand teams have around 2000 staff and I was humbled (and nervous) to be speaking to 150 of their leaders.

At the end of my talk, one of the company's senior executives pulled me aside and asked how many staff we had at the time, to which I said 25. He turned to another group of colleagues and said, "They had 25 staff and they did *that!*"

I was obviously wanting to make sure all the facts were correct and mentioned that when "we did that" (the Coles and Woolworths Campaign), we only had 10 staff. I could tell from the expressions on their faces that they were more than a little surprised.

That's when it dawned on me that there was a chance we didn't even fully understand the significance of what we'd done, and what we are doing. (These guys are sort of competitors but they could hear me speak at any conference, so I thought I'd head along just for fun and see what comes of it – I'll save the rest of this story for *Chapter Two*.)

MEASURING IMPACT, THEN AND NOW

We started from humble beginnings. But we kept going because we could see – and continue to see – what Thankyou will be. While it took us five years to raise just over $500,000 in project funding for causes that impact global poverty, now, having recently celebrated our seventh birthday, we have been able to give over $3.7 million dollars to our project partners.

By the time this book is in your hot little hands, that figure will be far greater as we've hit a tipping point. We have over 35 staff and over 35 products on the market (with many more about to launch), along with thousands of stockists and retail partners and ongoing media support. Thankyou received an estimated 50 million media impressions in financial year 2014 alone!

As an organisation, we've been lucky enough to be on the receiving end of a number of awards, including the 2013 and 2014 Social Traders Social Enterprise awards. Personally, there have been a couple of local and global awards floating around as well, which have given me a platform and the honour of being able to inspire others to chase their dreams.

The above sales figures, comments and even awards have been worth celebrating, but what's most exciting is that our impact is beginning to reach that all-important tipping point. It took us three years to fund safe water access for 2261 people (as at financial year 2011). Now, as at the time this book went to print in early 2016, we've been able to fund safe water access for over 190,000 people, along with hygiene and sanitation programs for over 302,000 people. We've also facilitated 19.1 million days' worth of access to short-term food aid, plus provided long-term food solutions and over 30,000 meals to disadvantaged Australians as part of our growing local impact.

The most exciting part for us is knowing this is just the beginning. As more Australians become aware of the range and make the switch, those numbers are going to grow exponentially into hundreds of thousands and then one day, millions of people.

THE POWER OF ONE

We believe that every person has value. Every person has an important story to live and every person has the right to access basic human rights like food and water. It's easy to get carried away with the numbers, the impact and even the comments from a few industry giants, but for us it always comes back to people.

I'll never forget one Monday morning when our team was in tears as Pete, our Chief Impact Officer, read out the story of Mrs A, one of our beneficiaries in northern Sri Lanka. Upon returning to her home after the war, having lost her husband and other relatives, Mrs A realised that accessing safe drinking water for her son and three daughters would become part of her daily struggle. The nearby wells had been badly damaged during the war, and the closest source of clean drinking water was a well 3km away near a military site – often a source of danger for the women and young girls who typically collect water for their families.

The war had left Mrs A with more than emotional scars. She had sustained a severe injury to her leg and hip. She could barely walk short distances around her village, let alone begin the 3km trek carrying water for her family. Faced with a terrible choice, Mrs A sent her oldest child to collect the family's fill of water. In July 2011, her 13-year-old daughter left home with her bike and jerry cans and began the journey as she'd done many times before. This time, she did not return.

Mrs A and her neighbours searched desperately for her daughter but found only her bike and water containers. A part of her torn dress was found in the bushes nearby. Like many women and girls who make the long journey in search of clean drinking water, Mrs A's daughter was never found.

In October 2012, Thankyou helped fund a well in Mrs A's community. When our water project partner visited Mrs A, she was overwhelmed by the impact the well would have on her community. With tears in her eyes she said, "If this well was built two years ago, my young daughter would still be with me now."

After hearing the story, we all sat in heavy silence. We never want to be two years too late again.

We are focused on making sure Thankyou becomes a household name. Why? It's not for bragging rights or to help us win another award. It's because at Thankyou, it's all about people. When we become that household name brand that is in literally millions of households, we'll be in a position to help millions of other people around the world.

GLOBAL DREAMS

Hands down, the number one question I am asked in public is, "Have you ever thought of taking Thankyou overseas?" This confirms for me the potential and global appeal of Thankyou. My usual answer to the question is a polite smile and reply that "one day we might get there". But the truth is, everything you've read – including the dollars raised, the products produced and the impact made – is nothing more than the initial building blocks in proving this concept.

We've proven that this idea can work to the point where products compete with major multinationals.

Thankyou is challenging the very foundation of the industry it operates in. Again, we've hit a tipping point.

Now the next set of building blocks in proving the concept is ascertaining whether the idea can launch in another country and scale. We've invited New Zealand to join us in this second part of our journey. From there? We'll let you dream with us. Our products are global products, and the issues they exist to solve are global issues.

Not to mention one small point: the plan from the very start was always to take this idea global. We've had to make some tough calls along the way as we set up something that has what it takes not just to 'go global', but to truly disrupt industries and make the biggest impact possible.

Will we get there? That's the million people, not dollar, question. The launch of this book is a risk, but we believe that it could work. The 'FutureFund by Thankyou' won't stop – it will continue to grow. Once our baby and toddler range is launched and New Zealand is launched, we cannot wait to announce our next funding milestones. We believe there will be a second and third chapter, and many more. How many 'chapters' do you think a good book should have?

AN OFFER TOO GOOD TO REFUSE... AND WE TURNED IT DOWN

At around the three-year mark of our journey, Jarryd, Justine and I had an experience that we won't soon forget. We met the CEO of a global convenience retailer and his leadership team, and they expressed interest in ranging Thankyou Water nationally through the United States.

This was a BIG deal! This group has nearly 10,000 stores in the US and over 50,000 stores globally.

One day, I'll talk more about the details of that meeting, but for now all I'll say is we were speechless. We couldn't believe what we were hearing. We couldn't believe the potential. Without question, this was our big moment...

But we never chased the opportunity. It was one of the toughest calls we have ever made, but we turned it down. At year three, we were nothing more than a bottle of water and while we believed that Thankyou was much more than that, we had yet to prove it.

We turned down this opportunity of a lifetime, for what? To spend the next two years developing 16 new products across three ranges, knowing that of the top 25 fast-moving consumer goods companies in the world, not one of them has the same brand operating across beverage, food and health and beauty categories. We were doing that, and trying to put together a marketing campaign that had no guarantee of working (our Coles and Woolworths Campaign).

We believed we had to prove the power of Thankyou – a brand built by people for people – first. A movement not built on a bottle of water but on an idea that could transcend any product. We've been building a model to scale.

Why didn't we attempt the US launch *and* develop the new product ranges and the campaign? There's a part of me that was dying because we were not attempting both, but I also recognised that one of our greatest assets is focus. We focused on Australia for two years and it played out almost exactly how we'd hoped and planned.

That offer was the first global offer, but it was not the last. Another opportunity came from a global CEO who I have the upmost respect for. His vision has achieved what no other young visionary has ever achieved. He's done what many have never been able to do and is one of the most inspiring people you could meet. His work inspired me to get to where I am today. The offer came with 'billionaire' backing, and included the ability to put our product into 14 countries. We declined; you'll see why in a few pages.

After the Coles and Woolworths Campaign, an offer came from a pair of the most inspirational CEOs I've ever come across, and who I also have the utmost respect for. The offer was remarkable. I am *still* speechless. Sitting with heroes, having a conversation I would never have expected was a mind-blowing experience.

For me, it was personally the hardest offer to decline, but our team believed that some of the conditions ultimately took away from the fundamental foundations of Thankyou. Were we being over-precious and over-protective? Did we miss another opportunity of a lifetime? Only time will tell. Sometimes, you have to take the risk to back what you feel in your heart, even if your rational mind is fighting it.

Later, we fielded interest from an influential UK CEO to get the rights to the Thankyou brand, along with a number of other global opportunities that kept knocking on our doors. My all-time favourite came after the Coles and Woolworths Campaign, when I had a missed call from Costco America on a Friday night. The voicemail, from an American voice, said, "We've been following your entire journey and want to discuss rolling all of your products into every Costco!"

I couldn't sleep all weekend. One of the largest retailers in the world wanted to launch all of our products? It was beyond our wildest dreams! I called back the number on Monday only to discover that my mate Mark, who now lives in the United States, had pranked me. He nailed the American accent and while I was a little upset, I had to admit it was a pretty good prank to pull. Mark, you have no idea what I'm planning to get you back for that.

Apart from Costco, each time an opportunity came up, we made the can't-even-put-into-words tough call not to take it. Why? Two reasons. The first is that each offer came with conditions that we knew would have given us scale overnight, but which diluted Thankyou's core philosophy. The second reason? Focus. While this myriad of opportunities were often tempting, we'd spent two and a half years focusing on solidifying our model to get ready for Chapter Two.

Chapter Two starts with the launch of this book and a call out to the people to help us expand into the baby and toddler market and into New Zealand to confirm the proof of concept of Thankyou – but that's just the beginning. Future funding targets and our plans for Thankyou will be outlined once (or if!) the first goals are achieved. Our vision is bold but we believe it's possible with your support.

10 OUT OF 10 EXPERTS WOULD SAY YOU'VE MADE A MISTAKE

I'd just finished speaking at an event a few nights before *Chapter One* went to print and as I walked off stage, I was introduced to a guy whom I was told had an incredibly impressive résumé in the start-up world.

His experience was definitely impressive. I was so excited! The more I found out about him, the more I couldn't wait to tell him about what we were doing. We sat down and he let me share about where we were at. Then, like any good person with experience, the questions started to flow.

"Why did you structure it to be owned by a charitable trust and lock out investors?" he asked. I was so excited to tell him it was because we exist 100 per cent for impact, but before I could finish, he challenged our model.

"How can you possibly scale?" he asked. I then got a quick schooling on how businesses scale globally, which was interesting and a little awkward, because we can't follow the same process according to the way start-ups tend to scale.

When I mentioned the US opportunity at year three, the pace in the conversation changed. I explained that we made a call to stay put in Australia and expand, rather than attempt to launch internationally before we were ready. He looked genuinely concerned as he told me that he sees this "all the time with start-ups, where people diversify too quickly." He went on to say that he felt we'd diversified too quickly and that we should have taken the opportunity to scale the water. In fact, it was his advice that we needed to pick up the phone and get that conversation going again immediately.

I protested with enthusiasm that this was all part of the plan; that we didn't want to scale a bottle of water, as we wanted to scale a much bigger idea. He told me, again, that we'd made a mistake, before questioning the expertise of our board and suggesting that we recruit some people who "actually know what they are doing".

He added that if he lined up 10 of his colleagues who have expertise in product (he named a few of the global companies they had each started or worked for), all 10 of them would tell us we'd made a huge mistake and need to go back and scale the water, not attempt food and other products.

He did make a throwaway comment that "perhaps you may show all of us to be wrong…"

Finally, he asked, "How many people die each day from water-related issues?" I told him it was 4500. "That's a big number!" he said, before commenting, "You realise you could have helped more people if you'd just scaled water years ago." He's not wrong. We could have.

We took a risk the day we decided not to chase those global water deals and instead, focused our efforts on building something the world hadn't seen before. But we did it believing that we could, in the long term, make a bigger impact than was possible with just a bottle of water. We won't know if that was the right call until many years from now.

At this point in the conversation, I thought I probably shouldn't discuss with him our grand plan of scaling the organisation through the consumer who has built the brand, by launching a sideways book at a 'pay what you want' price. It just didn't feel like the vibe was quite right!

As I walked away, a small, insecure part of me began questioning every major decision we'd made to date. I felt like I was completely in over my head. This guy wasn't a negative guy, saying nasty things. In fact, the last thing he said was really nice – that he'd open some doors for us if I reached out. He was a great guy sharing a lot of wisdom and insight and some really great points about scaling start-ups and ideas… But he was talking about the way they've always been successfully scaled. He had great examples of ways we could scale like others that are now billion-dollar companies, but our challenge is that we want to achieve something at Thankyou that is quite different to everyone else.

As I considered this conversation later, I realised something profound. When 10 out of 10 people think you've got it wrong, you probably do. Or, there's a chance that you are about to go on and do something the world hasn't seen before. The hardest part for me is hitting print on an idea publically, not knowing what the answer will be for us. But changing stuff was always going to be uncomfortable.

It's obvious we believe in an idea that not everyone can see yet, and on your journey you may face the same reality.

WHAT IS THANKYOU?

People didn't, and maybe still don't, fully understand that Thankyou is not just a bottle of water. It's not even a product range. It's not cause-related marketing or clever use of social media from a savvy marketing team, and it's not a business with a good social-giving component. It's not a fad, a trend or a little project that has gone better than expected. It can't be owned, purchased or taken over. Thankyou is a movement of people, which exists for people.

We exist because, at the time of writing, there are almost 1 billion people living in extreme poverty. We are on the journey with many other great organisations to reduce that figure – to zero!

What if each of us could play a part in eradicating global poverty through simply switching the brand of consumer products we buy every day?

Thankyou challenges the fabric of the global capitalist model and could empower billions of consumers to help end extreme poverty.

Thankyou's only major challenge is around scaling. Offers have come, but with conditions that compromise or distract from our foundation.

But what if the movement backed it? What if the people who purchased the products decided to scale Thankyou, not just to one country, but beyond? No conditions. No shares. No ownership. Just the freedom to make the biggest impact possible.

Well, I think that would be remarkable. I think that would change the world we live in forever.

SOME THOUGHTS TO TAKE AWAY

ONE. You must prepare for the 'what if it does work' scenario properly. If we could wind the clock back, we would have recruited more staff and been more prepared for a best-case scenario, to avoid overworking our team members.

TWO. Celebrate your successes – no matter how big or small. Don't just push through because there is more to do right now, as there will *always* be more to do.

THREE. David and Goliath's story is well known as pitching the underdog or the little guy against the giant. David took on Goliath with a sling and a few little stones, without armour, shields or swords. You probably don't have everything you are 'meant to have' on your journey, either. But what do your stones (unique ideas) look like? Others may not appreciate their potential, but it doesn't take as much as you think to bring down a giant. Look for the stones, not the traditional armour.

FOUR. Sometimes there is more power in your "no" than your "yes". Everything inside of us wanted to say "yes" to every opportunity, but by saying "no" in certain situations, we protected the value of the fundamentals that have brought us this far.

FIVE. "Jump in and learn how to swim later" is a tried and true strategy. You can't wait until you know it all before you take a leap. The only time you should rethink this is if you are literally jumping in the deep end in a pool and you don't know how to swim. In this case, I'd suggest you bring a buddy along – or at least wear some floaties.

CHAPTER 1.13
Choose Remarkable

"Don't close your eyes, this is your life.
Today is all you've got now, today is all you'll ever have."

In my early teenage years I heard these lyrics to a song by a US band called Switchfoot. On one hand, it was just a line from a song. But at the time, I interpreted it as a profound and inspirational statement.

You see, from an early age I had a first-hand understanding that tomorrow isn't guaranteed, and appreciated the fact that we must make the most of every day. My nanna, who I loved dearly, passed away from cancer at the age of 67. I was just 10 years old at the time and I can still remember our last goodbye; it was really hard to process that experience, knowing that the next day I couldn't go and see her again. It was a life-defining moment for me, and it wouldn't be my only one.

In my teenage years, every second Tuesday I would get picked up from school by some older guys in our community, along with some other friends from school. This group would invest time, encouragement and wisdom into us and we looked up to these older guys so much. In 2011, one of our group, Shaun, suddenly passed away. He was 26 years old and in the prime of his life. He'd been married for six months and was a much-loved husband, friend, son, brother and youth worker. Tragically, he died in a freak accident during a suburban game of Australian Rules Football. It was so sudden and so random.

In his relatively short life, Shaun made an incredible impact on so many people, myself included, because of the way he lived his life. He gave up his time for me and literally hundreds of other young people. The focus of his life as a youth worker was the pursuit of helping others. Most young guys don't do that; in fact few people live life with the goal of impacting others. There were literally thousands of people at his funeral.

I consider his life the definition of *remarkable*: for me it's life bigger than one's self, a life that positively impacted others. Thinking of his passing always reminds me that tomorrow is never guaranteed and motivates me to make every day bigger than just me, while always striving towards remarkable.

CHILDHOOD DREAMS

This is one of the reasons why I love speaking to primary school students – because to most of them, nothing is impossible. They are so excited about their dreams and so sure of their ability to be remarkable.

When you ask them what they dream of becoming, many light up as they explain their dreams of being a nurse, a doctor, a teacher, a mum, a dad, an astronaut, an artist, a singer, a dancer, an inventor, a pilot, a builder, a sportsperson representing their country... and the list goes on.

You could not (and would not want to) convince them that becoming anything they dream of is impossible. They live life believing they can be remarkable. Which of course, we all can. We just tend to forget this as we 'grow up'.

As we get older, we start to rank and rate what is remarkable and what is not. We teach each other to exist in those roles and we rarely dare to dream we could each be remarkable. Even as you read that list of childhood dreams, you probably held some choices in higher esteem than others. Could a mum and a prime minister both be truly remarkable? Can you really compare their impact? Maybe you should ask a prime minister's mother? Because without her dream to raise that child in the way she did, the prime minister's impact on the world may be very different.

If I were to look at some of those childhood dreams in the pursuit of remarkable, I would say this: Don't simply fly planes, fly people. John Flynn from the Royal Flying Doctors taught us that. Don't simply treat patients, transform people. Mother Teresa and Fred Hollows taught us that.

Don't simply paint a picture, cast a vision. Don't sing songs, create anthems. Don't dance to impress, dance to inspire. Li Cunxin who wrote *Mao's Last Dancer* taught us that.

Don't simply parent a child, prepare them for their destiny. My mum and dad taught me that. Don't teach a curriculum; inspire, equip and encourage your students to chase their dreams.

Don't simply manage people, unlock the potential inside them. I see that every day from the managers within Thankyou. Don't govern people, lead them. Nelson Mandela taught us that.

Don't just make or build things, build a legacy. Don't just create more of the same stuff, pioneer innovation. Steve Jobs taught us that. Don't go into business to create more money, create more change. Social entrepreneur Muhammad Yunus and philanthropist Bill Gates taught us that.

You have a choice – to simply exist, or to live a remarkable life, a life that's bigger than just you.

GIVING WHAT YOU CAN GIVE

I am fascinated by the thought that there are no two fingerprints the same, ever. It's almost impossible to comprehend. Keith Craft says, "You have a unique fingerprint that no one else has, to leave a unique imprint that no one else can leave." Ever since I first heard that statement I have been captivated by it.

I, too, believe that you have something remarkable to give that no one else can. At one of my speaking engagements sharing the Thankyou story I threw this question out there: "What if you could do something remarkable?" A guy yelled out in response that he would quit his job. The CEO called out in reply, "That's not the point of this session!" It was a funny and awkward moment, but it highlighted in a humorous way the trap that we can all fall into: thinking that we have to quit our job or make drastic changes to make a remarkable imprint.

You may want to do that, but my challenge to you is to think about how you can use your passion, skills, time, career, education and experience to live a life bigger than just you; a life that positively impacts others. This doesn't have to mean changing your entire life, but could mean doing what you already do, just in a new and impactful way.

Now I'm going to show you something over these next few pages at the risk of frustrating you. 'Don't frustrate the reader', 'you might care but no one else does', 'it's not important information' are all good points as to why I shouldn't include this, but if I don't show you you'll think a couple of people who started Thankyou are remarkable and that's it. Skip over it if you must but don't miss the point it should drive home to you.

There are a number of people we've encountered on our Thankyou journey who, at first glance, may seem like ordinary people doing ordinary things. But at some point, they've made the decision to do something remarkable, and the impact of that choice has helped deliver access to safe water, food and health and sanitation programs for hundreds of thousands of people.

For instance, I think Peter and Geoff are remarkable. They fly helicopters every day and decided one day that they'd donate their time to carry our sign to Coles and Woolworths.

I think that Daniel, Andrew, Vincent, Freya, Christian, Daniel, Andrew, Shobi, Eugene, James, Austin, Lora-Mae, Luke, Nathan, Nick, Alix, Taela, Sally, Bernadette, Paul, Kith and Sovannara are remarkable. Why? Because they film, colourgrade, edit and master television ads for a living, and one day they decided to donate over $110,000 of time and services to Thankyou to film our first-ever TV commercial.

I think Norma-Rose is remarkable. At the age of around 12, she got our products into her local independent supermarket. Like countless others who have managed to get Thankyou into their favourite stores, she did it by simply talking to the store manager.

And then there's John, Bill, Iain, Graham, Patrick, Brodie, Michelle, Greg, Gilda, Matt, Belinda, John, Gabe, Barry, Mark, Mauricio, Marcus, James, Ian, Emma, Margherita, Rachel, Claire, Marty, Samson, Kristi, Abby, Paul, Steve, Doug, Domenic, Joseph, Beatrice, Jules, the other James, Denise, Jarrod, Shiny, Anthony, Hanna, Tony, Chris and Honi. They're remarkable because they believed enough in what we were doing to get their companies and organisations behind our idea, by going above and beyond to provide services and resources – all of which helped us grow in some way.

I think Daniel, Shelley, Kim, Ailen, Nath, Jeremy, Ash, Chaemus, Dave, Adam, Simon, Tim, Jimi, Vanessa, Simon, Ian, John, Peter, Ash, Natalie, Cassandra, Lily, Thomas, Austin, Shannon, Nico, Sam, Doug, Jon, Andrew, Alvin and Gavin are remarkable. These guys gave their design, web-coding, videography, photography, sound-engineering, musical, catering, decorating, acting and other creative talents to help us implement our creative ideas and in doing so, spread the word about Thankyou.

And what about Jules, Chrissie, Ash, Scott, Andrew, Rebecca, Becca, Dean, Dylan, Poh, Tim, Liz, Nicole, Kate and Keiynan – who all remarkably used their celebrity influence to promote our Coles and Woolworths Campaign and make it a huge success?

Our current and past landlords – Steve, Peter, Duncan and Ash – have done remarkable things. They gave us office space that we couldn't afford at a price we could manage, all because they believed in what we were doing and wanted to be part of something greater.

A student called Nick is a remarkable guy. When he heard about Thankyou Water, he decided to get it stocked at his school. He also shared all of Thankyou's social media content online with his networks and one day, tweeted the prime minister about Thankyou, asking him to retweet it – and he did, reaching hundreds of thousands of people with our message.

Similarly, high school student Patricia is remarkable. She worked tirelessly to get Thankyou Water into her high school canteen – and not only that, inspired her entire school to back our organisation. Later, she became one of our most dedicated volunteers and because of her, there are a heap of people who know about Thankyou who didn't previously.

What Daizy, Jarrod, Nigel, Anastasya, Sophie, Olivia, Keely, Carol and so many others accomplished was remarkable. In their everyday lives, these guys engaged their communities and helped spread the word about Thankyou as our ambassadors – successfully getting our products into their local stores and school canteens.

A builder by the name of Paul, together with his mate Leigh, did something remarkable when they gave up their time and services to fit-out our first office for free. They even built our table tennis board table!

I think a lawyer called Adam, a partner at a law firm, who five years ago said, "I want to do your legal work for free" is remarkable. To this day we've never received a bill from him. His decision was worth tens or maybe even hundreds of thousands of dollars to us, and he achieved that by leveraging his everyday skills to do something remarkable.

It was remarkable how James, Vuki, Rob, Marija, Adam, Chris, Adam, Sarah, Karla, Abbey, Kate, Amanda, Kellie, Simon, Kate, Brianna, Izzy, Yuan and Simon decided to get behind us and provide pro bono and reduced-cost agency support, which helped us amplify our marketing and communications.

A young man by the name of Kirk did something remarkable when he dropped one day a week at work to volunteer with us, door knocking to get Thankyou Water into cafés. He had an MBA and probably should have been dedicating all of his time and energy towards taking the next step up in his career. But he made a choice based on something bigger than himself. I still remember standing on the ground with him in India, visiting one of the largest water projects we had funded to date, and seeing how proud he was at having been a part of doing something so remarkable.

The CEO, George, who simply said "yes" to having a 15-year-old kid follow him around for work experience for a week is remarkable. It was probably annoying for him and in fact, we'd all excuse George for declining the intrusion, considering his high-level role. But he made a decision to make an impact in a small but meaningful way. Little did he realise the impact that one week would have on my life.

I think Ralph, one of the first café owners who sold countless other products every day, is remarkable. He decided to sell our water and even told the Coke rep, who said he wanted Ralph to take our water out of their Coke fridge in his store, that they could put up with it, or take their fridge and their product with them.

And then there's Will, Tim, Flynn, Jeremy, Steve, Russell, Samantha, Neil, Leonie, Brad, Dean, Adam, Janine, Jono, Ian, Craig, Graeme, Craig, Naomi, Chad, Corey, Michael, Mike, Tracey, Pei Jet, George, Ai Jet, Francis and countless others – they're all remarkable. Every day they give people advice, based on their years of experience and wisdom. One day they decided to give Justine, Jarryd and I advice, because they believed in us and they believed in our cause. Our journey would have been very different without their input.

There's Adam, David, Nuala, Michael, Dan, Monica, Michael, Mike, Nick, Carrie, Caitlin, Aj, Cara, Eliza, David, Rebecca, Erin, Jackie, Nadia, Lisa, Claire, Tara, Rose, Sarah, Mia, Lucy, Lorna, Jane, Justine, Linda, Tim, Penny, Justine and Emma – these guys are remarkable. Every day, they work in the media industry and cover various stories, yet they chose to cover us multiple times and helped to spread the word about Thankyou.

I think Rod is remarkable. He drives digital billboard trucks. One morning he woke up and although he had never heard of our organisation before, within hours of learning about us, he decided to back our movement. Based on an overnight groundswell of support for our products, he decided to drive his digital billboard truck out the front of the Virgin Australia head office, showcasing our products – for free.

I think Dani, Lucy, Nellie, Rebecca, Ina, Emily and Nadia are remarkable. These bloggers used their influence to spread the word about Thankyou.

Kevin, Nath, Ruth, Travis, Matt, Belinda, James, Josh, Blake, Samuel, Rita, Robert, Travis, Alexandra, Dean, Justin, James, Justin, Adam, Dean, Eliza, Lukas, Jannah, Jessica, Kathryn, Ruth, Helen, Jono, Travis, Shannon, Mary, Lisa, Laura, Joy, Jonathan, Catherine, Roz, Morello, Aneeka, Wesley, Rowena, Nick, Lisa, Kate, Jody, Jeanette, Romy, Kristen, Sean and Catherine have shown us remarkable support. These guys and countless others spent hours recording a song, skit or other creative videos to help products get ranged in supermarkets.

I think Jarryd, Justine, Morgan, Nicolette, Craig, Graeme, Pete, Sarah, Callum, Joel, Kirk, Wesley, Jan-Lee, Bethany, Hannah, Steph, Tim, Melissa, Jess, Tom, April, Rebecca, Tom, Joanna, Alana, Elizabeth, Julia, Nicole, May-threen, Travis, Ashley, Rebecca, Lydia, Kara, Vincent, Robin, Rachel, Lily, Benson, Benjamin, Ishara, Nadine, Laura, Lucy, Kai, Emily, Amanda, Benjamin, Michael, Lauren, Jess, Steve, Christoph, Adam, Simon, Louisa, Caitlyn and Marina are remarkable. One day they chose to give up part of their working life to a cause bigger than themselves, and that's how they ended up on our team.

I think Jim is remarkable. He sold SMEG fridges for a living, yet one day he decided to donate probably the coolest black SMEG fridge you've ever seen to our lunchroom. He even paid for the shipping!

And there's a remarkable bunch of people, who include Eleanor, Vanessa, Daniel, Arlana, Vishesh, Naomi, Patricia, Duc, Jia, Jolene, Tim, Shelley, Paul, Leigh, Merryn, Will, Pete, Dave, Queenie, Jason, Dave, James, Nath, Matt, Bell, Jeremy, Jono, Ash, Lauretta, Tim, Pete, Kirk, Wesley, Lily, Simon, Tom, Kim, Shobi, Brendan, Catherine, Carolyn, Andrew, Stephany, Matt, Russ, Lauren, Bec, Gavin, Hudson, Brooke, Alicia, Russell, Sienna, Rocky, Tarini and David – and many others. Over the years, they have volunteered or given up their time or resources in some capacity to build our organisation. They had careers, university and many other commitments, yet they decided to give their time to volunteer for a cause bigger than themselves.

Then there are the tens of thousands of diehard supporters who have not only purchased our products, but also spent their time spreading the word through their schools, universities, workplaces, community groups and online platforms.

And there are those people who have financially supported us to get us to where we are today, for which we're so incredibly grateful.

I didn't keep a list and my memory isn't recalling every name of those who have donated time, talent and money to the Thankyou cause since our journey began in 2008. There are many more remarkable people who have contributed than I could possibly list, and if I have forgotten anyone I truly apologise; your generosity was deeply felt.

Generally speaking, the people who have built the foundations of Thankyou don't stand on stages or appear on television, and a movie may not ever be made about them. But their names are crafted into this book because using their skills, talent, time, ability and passion, their contribution has helped to change the lives of individuals, families and communities for generations to come. They made a choice to do something bigger than themselves. They made a choice to be remarkable.

Each of them used their own unique fingerprint to leave a unique imprint. The result is the book you are holding and the impact that Thankyou has had on literally hundreds of thousands of people living in global poverty.

That's why my challenge to you is simple: *find a way*. A way to use your talent, your passion, your time, your ideas and your resources to make an impact outside of just you. It will look different for everyone, as you've seen in reference to the Thankyou journey, but I believe it's achievable for every single person in our world.

SO *THIS* IS WHAT GREATNESS LOOKS LIKE...

One Thursday evening I messaged one of my mentors. "I should have texted you earlier; I'm really struggling," I wrote.

First thing the next morning, he was at our office. We sat on our office rooftop and I ran him through where I was and why I was struggling, mentally. We had faced four major challenges in one week. Each was big enough on its own to really rock our organisation, but combined they seemed completely overwhelming. We were being forced to make some really tough calls and personally I was finding it hard.

As my mentor left me that Friday, he said something I'll never forget. With a grin on his face he said, "Daniel, remember, this is what greatness looks like; never forget it."

The previous night, long after decisions had been made, I found myself in my room curled up with intense cramps. I tried taking a few different medications but nothing worked – the stress had affected me physically in a way it never had before.

Seven days later, after that moment in my room, I was in Germany with Jarryd, where I was honoured to receive a global award as one of 'The JCI Ten Young Outstanding Persons of the World'. I went back to my hotel that night and couldn't sleep; my mind was ticking over and I got up and wrote a blog article, with a picture of the 10 award recipients on stage attached. I titled it, "This is what greatness looks like (and it's not what you think)".

I opened the blog by saying that we live in a society that equates greatness with a moment of success, such as that image from the awards, but I'd like to suggest a different perspective.

I shared the details of that moment one week earlier, where I was lying on the floor in pain, and then the conversation the next morning with my mentor. I shared his words, which have stuck with me to this day – that this is what greatness looks like.

I believe each of us can choose remarkable and can walk in greatness every day and in fact, most of us do – it just looks a little bit different to how society paints it. The greatness can be found in a humbling, uncomfortable and at times a very lonely process.

THE PROCESS

I can sum up the process of our entire Thankyou journey in 10 steps, which can literally be applied to anything, from business ideas to new parenting techniques.

I wish I could give you something that was a little more technical and made me look a lot smarter than I am, but I can't – because making your dreams a reality, changing stuff, challenging the status quo and leaving that unique imprint on the world isn't as complicated as you may believe.

TEN STEPS

one. Have thought or idea
two. Seek counsel (advisors)
three. Take action
four. Fail
five. Learn
six. Refine thought or idea
seven. Take action
eight. Repeat steps two to seven until you find yourself at step nine
nine. Succeed
ten. Enjoy and repeat

It's generic, but it works. I've tried and tested it many times, for many years. So too has nearly every person who's created or changed *anything*. As simple as this process is for me personally, it's led to an extremely fulfilling life.

Step one, having a thought or idea, is the starting point. Step two, seeking counsel (getting advice) is so important but as I state in earlier chapters, there is wisdom in seeking out a multitude of counsellors. Most people stop at step two after they've received some advice. Step three is the scariest step you'll ever take, especially when the advice you received may not have been as positive as you were hoping. Step four, 'fail', is one of the most important. Learn to fail fast. It's our story and the story of everyone who I've ever met who has succeeded.

Step five will be the difference between stalling perpetually and reaching step ten. A good friend of mine, Andy, once said over breakfast, "Leadership is learning, but in front of more people." It's an incredibly profound statement and reminds me that learning isn't for the beginners, it's for everyone and it's continual. Learn fast. Step six, refine thought or idea, speaks of continual refinement. It's a Thomas Edison moment and it's about finding the "10,000 ways that won't work".

Steps seven and eight require you to find more courage than any of the previous steps. It's a courage that most people are never prepared to find. What most people don't realise is that if you can make it to step seven, you are so close to success, even though most days you'll feel so far away.

Step nine doesn't need a lot of explanation but if you asked me three or four years into our journey what step ten was, I would have gotten the answer wrong. I would have said it was just "repeat", not "enjoy and repeat". After meeting that investment banker, I realised how important it is to actually stop and enjoy the wins before you repeat the process.

Could making your ideas and dreams a reality be as simple as following ten steps? Could you really change stuff and live a remarkable life from what appears to be an incredibly generic process?

Yes.

Is it really that easy?

No.

If it was, I could have cut the 65,000 or so words out of this book and only published 'The Ten Steps'. What's the point of including it all? Because we need more than steps and more than a process. Robots follow processes well, but for us people, our humanity gets in the way.

This book is designed to be more than a 'How to succeed' type of manual. Instead, we aim to show you 'How to stick at the process' to make your dreams and ideas a reality, with many real life examples to add weight to the words. The stories and lessons we've learned, I hope, will inspire you and equip you practically to stick with the process.

I've completed those ten steps a few times before. Right now, you are holding in your hand step three, 'take action'. This whole book isn't a 'success story', it's a 'step three' story that I hope will inspire you to start your own process.

I'll hit those ten steps again and again. Will you?

WHAT'S STOPPING YOU?

There's usually just one thing stopping you from working through the above process. It's got you locked up from choosing the remarkable. Put simply – it's an excuse.

I meet so many people who share their dreams with me. They are just waiting until they've finished their degree, landed a secure job, or made some good progress in their career before they execute it. Or they're holding off until they have some savings behind them, or some other back-up plan.

Maybe having a back-up plan is taking the responsible approach. As a university dropout who had no experience, no savings, no secure job and no plan B, all I can tell you is this: sometimes, having nothing to fall back on can work in your favour. Also, we live in a world full of very safe and responsible people who are not living their dreams and are simply 'existing'. Which would you rather be?

Only two things are certain in this life: birth and death. Everything in between is yet to be decided. Your life isn't simply a product of the hand that you were dealt, it's also a product of the decisions you make.

There were many excuses we could have legitimately made since launching Thankyou and if we opted for those 'easy outs', we would have stayed exactly where we were. Had we made those choices, this story would not exist today. We were too young, too inexperienced, too busy, we didn't have any money behind us... We have grown up a little, but I still catch us making excuses around budget or resources or other challenges every now and then. It can be hard to stop making excuses. So, let me tell you a story that constantly inspires me to avoid them.

First, I'm going to ask you a question. Put up your hand right now – and I mean actually physically raise your arm in the air, right now – if you are aged 12 years or older? If you do, I promise you'll remember this moment for the rest of your life. (You can put your hand down now.)

At the age of 12, my cousin Ben decided that he wanted to make a difference and sponsor a child. He didn't receive pocket money or have a job. At this point most of us would accept that it's just not feasible for him to sponsor a child. We wouldn't even call these excuses, we'd call them legitimate reasons for a 12-year-old to not sponsor a child. But Ben didn't let these things stop him and instead, he started his own dog walking enterprise to raise the money he needed.

I know what you're thinking. This is a cute idea that might have lasted about a week – a month at best. That's probably what a lot of Ben's friends and family thought at the time, too. But after a few weeks, Ben was walking multiple dogs. He had his own business cards and pamphlets and it wasn't long before he was walking over a dozen dogs per week. It got to the point where he was paying his friends an hourly rate to walk dogs on his behalf, while he still made a tidy profit for his projects, of course!

Ben went on to sponsor seven children. He also fully-funded a well in India for a whole community to get access to safe water, and he recently funded a microfinance program for 10 women to start their own sewing business. He's raised over $18,000 for his projects. Be inspired by Ben's story – inspired to not let *any* excuse (often disguised as legitimate and logical reasons) stop you.

NO SMARTER THAN YOU

When Justine and I watched the movie *Jobs*, about the life of Apple founder Steve Jobs, one particular statement from the movie stood out to both of us:

"Life can be much broader once you discover one simple fact, and that is: everything around you that you call life, was made up by people that were no smarter than you. And you can change it, you can influence it, you can build your own things that other people can use."

We felt like we knew exactly what he was talking about as it summed up our entire journey. If I had heard this quote before launching Thankyou, I would have just said to myself, "Yeah, that's fine for you to say, because you're Steve Jobs." But we've learned from experience that his statement was both profound and, ultimately, true. Each of us truly does have the power to change stuff.

I hope in the openness of our failures and our journey that you can see what is possible for your life and realise that you have a contribution to make, too. The fact is, your contribution counts, no matter how big or small.

When you consider that there are over 7 billion people in our world, it's very easy to feel insignificant.

But can I ask you to consider this? Right now, think about the fact that in the entire history of humankind there has only ever been, and will only ever be, one <write your full name>
_____   <and your date of birth>.
                born on

You made it to the last chapter of this book because there is a part in you that believes you've got something remarkable to offer the world. Remarkable is defined in the dictionary as "worthy of attention". It does not necessarily mean "will be turned into a movie or a book". For some of you, your stories might be movie material, but that's not the measure of remarkable.

Don't get caught up in the numbers. We learned that lesson on the first trip to Cambodia, back when we mistakenly believed that just because we'd 'only' made an impact on a few people, the value of that impact was diminished. Every person has a story, every story has value and if we could all help just one other person, our world would look remarkably different.

What dream are you living out? What ideas will you make a reality? What game will you be part of changing? What imprint will you leave?

Winston Churchill said, "History will be kind to me, because I intend to write it."

Our story isn't over yet, and I get the feeling that neither is yours. So to the dream chasers, game changers, status-quo breakers:

Write hard, write fast*.

---

* Note: Don't be afraid to flip what you write horizontal and then publish it globally, just because no one else has succeeded at it before. Like Shayne, Scott and Josh at LS Travel Retail confirmed, as they ranged a world-first book concept in under 24 hours, "If we are going to change the game, we are going to have to think differently." I couldn't have said it any better myself.

You have the power to change stuff.

WHAT WILL WE TELL OUR GRANDCHILDREN?

At 1pm on Monday July 6, 2015, our team welcomed our newest intake of interns. A question went out over email from Jess in our People & Culture team, prepping everyone to share with the interns their answer to: "What would you tell your grandchildren one day about the team at Thankyou?" Justine and I couldn't make the meeting because at 1.30pm that day, while the meeting was in full swing, we were busy welcoming our first son, Jedediah Daniel Flynn, into the world.

The thought I had for the interns, which I later emailed, was this: "It is my hope to one day tell Jed's kids that we used to live in a world where people once didn't have access to basic human rights, like clean water, food, education, adequate health and sanitation, and I got to be part of a team, part of a consumer movement that played a small but significant role in ending that. It is my hope to one day read a book to my children's children. Not a book that I wrote, but a book that we wrote. Who is 'we'? We were a couple of kids in university, then a few more joined and 'we' became hundreds, then 'we' became thousands, then 'we' became hundreds of thousands, then 'we' became millions and soon hundreds of millions of people. Each of us writing the part of the story that we could, some big, some small, but all significant, even down to those who made a single purchase."

An older gentleman once asked a young boy why he bothered to pick up starfish and throw them back into the ocean. He pointed out to the young boy that there were probably millions of starfish stuck on the beach and said, "What difference could you possibly make to this problem?" The boy picked up another starfish, threw it back into the ocean and said, "I just made a difference for that one."

I've said it before and I'll say it again: As I write this book, there are almost 1 billion people living in extreme poverty. We believe in a world where extreme poverty shouldn't be a reality for anyone.

Thankyou is an opportunity for each of us to ensure we live in a world where people are empowered with access to basic human rights like water, food, sanitation and hygiene training.

It's an opportunity for each of us to play a part in eradicating global poverty. Join us.

WANT TO SUPPORT THANKYOU FURTHER?

We all have the power to change stuff – maybe you want to change something in your life or maybe you want to impact the lives of others. Either way, chasing your dreams will have a huge impact on this world.

Every now and then people's dreams collide with what we're trying to do with Thankyou and they ask how they can help us grow and create a bigger impact. If you're asking this too, here's a few ways you can help us make a difference:

✎ Help launch Chapter Two

You might run an organisation, teach at a school, own a retail business, run a university, be part of a community group or maybe you're one of those people who loves connecting great ideas with great people. Help us reach a tipping point by putting this book – this story, this idea – into the hands of others in your sphere of influence. You might purchase three copies, 30 copies or 30,000 copies but whatever you decide, know that you're taking Thankyou one step closer to that tipping point. You can follow updates and contribute to the FutureFund by heading to: *thankyou.co*

◇ Join a movement of world-changing consumers

Buying our products is an obvious step, but there are other extremely powerful ways that you as a consumer can help Thankyou grow.

Talk to your local café, supermarket or retail store manager about stocking Thankyou products.
Products get store ranging because consumers ask for them! Trust me, you as a consumer have more power than you realise.

If you notice a Thankyou product disappear from the shelf, ask for it back.
At the end of the day, retail buyers make the final call about whether to stock or take products off shelves. So if you see another product in the spot where your favourite Thankyou item used to sit, let your local store know that you want Thankyou back. Just think, one family with a grocery bill of $300 a week will spend $15,600 a year. That's a whole lot of buying power for stores to listen to.

Tidy up Thankyou products on the shelf while you're doing your weekly shop.
Nearly every product company pays third-party companies to walk around the shops for them, straightening the product and making sure that it has the correct shelf space. We had a third-party company working with us for a while, but then we made the decision to drop them so we can maximise our dollars for impact. With your help, we can keep our products looking awesome on the shelf, which makes them stand out amongst our competitors and helps more customers find our products. It takes about three seconds of time, but simple actions can make a remarkable difference.

Join a movement of world-changing retailers and distributors

Each of our retailers and distributors has always sold great products. But the day they started selling Thankyou products, they began to make a serious global impact. If you are a retailer or distributor of consumer products and want to stock Thankyou products in your stores or warehouses, then please get in touch with the team by contacting *info@thankyou.co.*

Word of mouth eats billboards for breakfast

Your help to spread the word about Thankyou is powerful. Tell your friends about Thankyou and the power of making the switch in the products they buy. Connect with us and let us keep you updated as we continue along our journey. Our greatest breakthrough moments have come through the support of our incredible social media community who have backed our campaigns. Our past campaigns are just the beginning, and our biggest are yet to come.

We hope you'll be part of it!

LET'S BE FRIENDS

Follow updates by signing up to Thankyou's e-newsletter, *The Latest*, by heading to *thankyou.co* or dropping a line to *thelatest@thankyou.co*

Thankyou

f **Ⓟ** @thankyouaus / @thankyounz

🐦 @thankyou_aus

Daniel Flynn

Ⓟ @danielflynn88 / **Ⓣ** @danielmflynn

Search '*Thankyou YouTube*' to watch videos from the journey

The curious part in us seriously can't wait to see people reading this book the 'wrong way around'!

Share your *Chapter One* reading moment with us **#chapterone**

Thankyou's home – our warehouse office in Collingwood, Melbourne. The two brothers who own the building gave us a crazy rate we could actually afford. It's ordinary people like this who have helped build the Thankyou movement.

Jarryd, myself and Justine in our offices. We had no idea this photo was being taken, obviously.

EARLY DAYS

From the moment we stood in front of the very first bottles of Thankyou Water to purchasing our items from the supermarket, it's been a crazy ride. When Justine, Jarryd and myself visited the very first food program funded through our food range it was a beautiful reminder of how important the work we support is, and that there is still so much work to do.

OUR CAMPAIGNS

As part of our Coles and Woolworths Campaign, we flew a couple of giant 10,000 square foot signs (the signs were generously donated while the helicopter pilots gave up their time!) over Coles' and Woolworths' head offices at around 8.30am above peak-hour traffic. That was a fun day. Oh, and there was the impromptu campaign to get Thankyou products stocked on Virgin Australia flights by printing our message to Sir Richard Branson on a digital billboard on the side of a truck. We're nothing if not bold.

MR KEM VOUN IS A MAN OUR TEAM WON'T FORGET

Having lost his leg in the Cambodian Civil War, Mr Kem Voun used to rely on others for so much and his children would sometimes leave school early to help him. "My family was in poverty, I lacked many things," Mr Voun said. This changed when Mr Voun took hold of the opportunity to be involved in an agricultural community program that we funded. Because of Mr Voun's determination and drive, he was able to gain access to training and financial support, and has now increased his family's livelihood to build a stable future.

THIS IS THE INCREDIBLE CHRISTINE

Meet Christine: farmer, mother and savvy entrepreneur. "My life has changed..." she said, as she took us through her sewing shop. Christine took part in a food program we funded, that provided her with agricultural training which helped her transform her farm into a thriving business. Christine now has 144 orange trees, 100 paw-paw trees and 25 mango trees with the profits helping to feed her family, send her kids to school and launch a new business venture – the sewing shop – to support them in the off-season.

A group of women in Assam, India, teaching Justine some traditional Indian dance moves.

THIS IS DEBRA

"
The day I first got into the toilet was the happiest day of my life...
"

When we funded the implementation of a latrine with wider door frames, hand rails and ramp access in a Zimbabwean community, it was the first time that 12-year-old Debra was empowered to use the bathroom unassisted. "I can use it well without any hindrance," said Debra.

With her dignity and confidence restored, Debra's dreams extend far into the future. "I want to be a teacher when I grow up, because I want to teach everything that's done in this school."

> " A good life is not only for me, but for the community and also my children and in the future. "

MEET ROMALDO

Until recently, Romaldo and his family in Timor Leste carefully planned how much water they'd need each day because it was a 10km mountainous trek to fetch more. We funded a water project in Romaldo's community, and now things are different. Not only were Romaldo and many from his community instrumental in the process of building the project, but they were also empowered to maintain the solution long term. "I've never had any formal education, but with courage and confidence I can do all these things."

One of the most significant moments for me in our journey – going on a water walk with 15-year-old Vianney in Burundi.

This was the brand-new gravity fed water system that we funded, which meant Vianney no longer had to walk a long uphill trek each day to access safe water – it was just metres from his front door.

The above photo was one of the first images we ever took in the field during a trip to Cambodia in 2010. Meeting this woman and seeing the difference between her old water source and the purified water she had received through our funding was a defining moment (and a reality check) for us all.